How to . . .

get the most from your
COLES NOTES

Key Point
Basic concepts in point form.

Close Up
Additional hints, notes, tips or background information.

Watch Out!
Areas where problems frequently occur.

Quick Tip
Concise ideas to help you learn what you need to know.

Remember This!
Essential material for mastery of the topic.

Moms and Dads' Guide to . . .

Soccer for Kids

League and age divisions

How to help out at home

Rules and strategies

COLES NOTES have been an indispensable aid to students on five continents since 1948.

COLES NOTES now offer titles on a wide range of general interest topics as well as traditional academic subject areas and individual literary works. All COLES NOTES are written by experts in their fields and reviewed for accuracy by independent authorities and the Coles Editorial Board.

COLES NOTES provide clear, concise explanations of their subject areas. Proper use of COLES NOTES will result in a broader understanding of the topic being studied. For academic subjects, Coles Notes are an invaluable aid for study, review and exam preparation. For literary works, COLES NOTES provide interesting interpretations and evaluations which supplement the text but are not intended as a substitute for reading the text itself. Use of the NOTES will serve not only to clarify the material being studied, but should enhance the reader's enjoyment of the topic.

© Copyright 1998 and Published by
COLES PUBLISHING. A division of Prospero Books
Toronto - Canada
Printed in Canada

Cataloguing in Publication Data
Fairfield, Shelley, 1965–

Moms and Dads' guide to—soccer for kids: league and age divisions;
how to help out at home, and rules and strategies

ISBN 0-7740-0569-6

1. Soccer for children.   I. Title.   II. Series

GV944.2.F34 1998   796.334'083   C98-930455-8

Publisher: Nigel Berrisford
Editing: Paul Kropp Communications
Book design and layout: Karen Petherick, Markham, Ontario
Character development: Michael Petherick
Illustrations: Michael Petherick and Eileen Sweeney

Manufactured by Webcom Limited
Cover finish: Webcom's Exclusive DURACOAT

Contents

CHAPTER ONE

The rules of soccer in a nutshell

Soccer is the most popular game in the world. In the harshest climates, in the poorest slums, in the richest principalities, across oceans, ages, abilities and genders, soccer reigns supreme. Legendary players of the game started in the streets, playing barefoot and using a ball made of rags or other pieces of scrap leather. It is a game that requires virtually no equipment, no money and no special training to grasp. It's much more comfortable for the players if they have all those things, but for the die-hards, luxuries don't really matter. All kids need is a space, a ball and a little bit of time ... and the game is on!

HOW THE GAME IS PLAYED

Soccer is a simple game to learn. It's played with two teams of 10 players on the field and a goalkeeper whose job is to guard against goals attempted by the other team. The 10 players spread out on the soccer field against the opposing players and try to win possession of the ball long enough to score a goal on the other team. A goal is scored when the ball is kicked between the goalposts and under the crossbar at either end of the field. Possession of the ball may only be won and kept by using the feet, legs, head and upper body. Any use of the arms or hands to control the ball (or other players) is not allowed.

To start the game, the ball is placed at center field and the two opposing teams line up on either side of the half line. The team that wins the coin toss kicks off. Then players attempt to dribble and pass the ball around to their teammates so that the ball goes close enough to the other team's goal, or net, to kick, knee, head or otherwise push (except with the hands) the ball across the goal line. Once a goal is scored, play stops. The ball is returned to center and the team that was scored against kicks off.

The game is governed by time and the rules. The adult game takes 90 minutes to play, and consists of two 45-minute halves. Kids' games are usually under an hour, with the time divided into halves. There is usually one referee who keeps the official time and watches the players to make sure they don't break the rules. If they do, the referee will usually blow a whistle and play will stop. The team that breaks the rules loses possession of the ball. Play restarts when the ball is kicked into play by the other team.

WHO PLAYS WHERE

The 11 players on a team have different positions. One of them is goalkeeper. Others are defenders, halfbacks (midfielders) and forwards or "strikers." There are other positions in more sophisticated play, but for the most part players play on one of those three lines.

THE PLAYING FIELD

The playing field in soccer may vary in size, but the markings are always the same. There are goal lines on the ends of the field, touch lines down the sides, a halfway line and a 44 x 18 yard rectangle (called the penalty area) and a 20 x 6 yard rectangle (the goal area) at both ends of the field. The goals sit on the center of each of the goal lines, with the posts measuring eight yards apart and eight feet high. At each of the four corners of the field is a corner area marked by a flag and a quarter circle of one yard radius.

One mark that is supposed to be there, and probably won't be on a kids' field, is the penalty mark. It is a spot that sits 12 yards out from the goal, and is the designated spot for taking penalty kicks. If a penalty kick is called, and there is no spot marked on the field, the referee will walk out from the goal 12 yards or "steps" and put the ball on the ground. The last mark on the field is a semicircle 10 yards further out from the penalty spot. This is supposed to show where opposing players must stand until the ball is kicked (but it probably won't be there either, so the referee estimates the 10 yards, just as he does on all other free kicks).

2

The soccer field

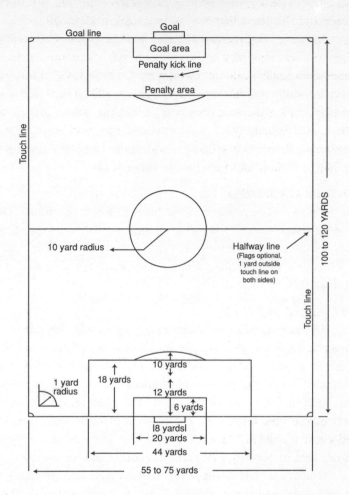

Goal line
Goal
Goal area
Penalty kick line
Penalty area
Touch line
10 yard radius
Halfway line
(Flags optional,
1 yard outside
touch line on
both sides)
Touch line
100 to 120 YARDS
10 yards
18 yards
12 yards
6 yards
1 yard
radius
|8 yards|
← 20 yards →
← 44 yards →
← 55 to 75 yards →

In case you were wondering why everything is measured in yards, it is because the rules of the game originated in Britain, and have been stuck to faithfully.

In terms of what is not allowed on a soccer field, there is really one guiding principle: as long as the players are playing the ball, the play is legal. As soon as they start to play the body (or "the man") it's a foul. If a play seems like not a very nice thing to do, it is probably against the rules. However, there is a strange rule in soccer that lets players get away with committing fouls and it's called the play-on rule. If a player is fouled but manages to maintain control of the ball or keeps on developing the attack despite the foul, the referee will call "play on." It's a judgement call, and it's always controversial, but it's all part of the excitement of this sport.

The rules of soccer are universal and governed by an organization called FIFA (the Fédération Internationale de Football Association). With the exception of mini-soccer, the rules do not change according to the age or ability of the players. The professionals are governed by the same set of rules as the twelve-year-old novices. The only variations you and your child are likely to encounter are the regulations surrounding field size, number of players needed to play a game, substitutions during a game (when, how and how many players may be substituted) and the length of the game. You will need to check with your own league to see how its regulations differ from FIFA regulations.

WHAT YOU CAN EXPECT TO SEE

If this is your child's first summer of soccer, you've both got a huge learning experience ahead of you. This book is written to help you know what to expect, or at least be prepared for, as your child gets involved in a new sport.

Let's start with the brand-new player, and the first game she will ever play. She is probably between the ages of six and nine, and has a vague idea that she has to run around a field and kick a ball. It looks and sounds like great fun – everybody charging around, getting lots of exercise, developing social skills. And it is! So what are you looking at when you first get to the field? Every child on the field with the same idea: "I should run my hardest and fastest, and get to the ball first, and then kick it! And then run, and kick it again, until I can kick it into the net!" A-plus for enthusiasm, certainly, but there's one flaw, and that is there's only one ball.

Well, that doesn't seem to prevent kids from trying. As a result you get beehive soccer, where there's a great unruly mob surrounding the ball, hacking and thrashing up and down the field. There are probably fouls happening all over the place, but the sheer number of bodies and limbs is so dense no referee can see them. Amid the melee, the ball is kicked back and forth until it eventually squirts loose. A great charge downfield ensues, with everyone running full tilt. The most coordinated and fastest player gets to the ball first. He hammers the ball as hard as he can, probably with his toe, and chases after it as fast as he can, with the rest of the scrum behind him. And so it goes until the ball goes out-of-bounds, or gets near the goalkeeper.

Now, at this stage of development, everyone usually has to take turns playing in net. The coach takes aside the designated goalkeeper for the day before each game and impresses upon her that her job is to stay in the net and prevent the other team from scoring a goal. She can do that by kicking the ball away, or by picking it up with her hands. Sometimes the coach even explains what to do after that, but usually the goalkeeper forgets. So, some poor child is standing in this enormous net, a sitting duck, while the fastest and most coordinated kid leads the mob downfield right at her. There can be nothing more terrifying to the average eight-year-old than this sight. The designated goalkeeper's adrenaline starts to pump. She starts to shuffle her feet along the goal line. She may start to jump up and down, then crouch over, eyes wide. She hears the thunder of 40 feet bearing down on her, the ball lurching from side to side, bounding mercilessly with heavy top spin across the turf, and into the goal area.

And so, what usually happens is one of two things. Your young goalkeeper remains firmly on the goal line, protecting her turf, stalwart in her defenses, and silently praying that the toe shot coming will miss the net (and her) entirely, or will be blocked by another in the swarm, or will somehow be muffed very badly so that it trickles softly right into her hands. The other possibility lies in your goalkeeper getting quite aggressive, and stepping off the goal line, running directly into the mob to get the ball before they can crush her. Either proposition is to be dreaded and so most of the time in eight-year-old soccer, the goalkeeper is completely irrelevant. The best parents, coaches and players can hope for is the development of a deep and abiding respect for the position of goalkeeper, and indoctrinating the ethic of avoiding bone-crushing contact with him or her.

Having said that, the mob more than likely will run the goalkeeper over and converge along the goal line, where the ball will be kicked very hard off the mass of bodies until it crosses the line, and a goal is scored. The ball will then be retrieved by one of the defensive players as the goalkeeper picks herself up, wipes the grit from her eyes and plants herself on the line again, waiting for the next assault. The rest of the players go back to their original starting positions – forwards, halfbacks or defenders, and prepare to kick off again.

Did someone say starting positions? What a novel concept – playing positions! It seems that kids just can't manage to play positions until they are 11 or 12. So, the very same team that played as a beehive just two short seasons earlier can actually manage to stay away from the ball long enough to introduce the concept of the pass. From the opening kickoff, then, instead of thundering the ball up the field as far as it will go, and a full-scale charge after it, the very same team may try a short forward pass to another player, who may then decide, calmly and efficiently, to pass the ball to a third player, who will try to control the ball and either dribble, or pass off again to a fourth player, and so on. This is the essence of soccer – the ability to calmly use space and skills and the mind to control the ball, rather than having the ball control everything, is the absolute aim of advanced soccer players. The transformation from killer bee to savvy play-maker can be long and arduous, but with the right attitudes, the right coaching and real enthusiasm for the game, it can and will happen.

CHAPTER TWO

The basic skills

In the early beehive stage of soccer there isn't a lot going on that really resembles a soccer game, with one very important exception. All the kids in the beehive are focusing on playing the game, and are concentrating very hard on the most critical single item in a game – the ball. This initial swarm stage is very important in developing the proper mental outlook and level of focus required to play soccer later on. Often there are children who disengage from the pack and wander off in the middle of the game to pick dandelions or braid each other's hair. If this is your child, there is still hope, but he or she needs encouragement to be more mentally involved in the game. While sitting on the sidelines children should be encouraged to watch their teammates, and to study the kicking and passing techniques used by them. They should be encouraged to understand what makes a good play – and what makes a really dumb play – as the game is in progress. Staying alert to where people are on the field, and where the ball is at all times is really the most critical aspect of the game. It's this mental edge that can make a player with average skills a very effective teammate.

Making the transition – from bee-dom to freedom

In order to separate from the pack, several skills beyond focusing must be developed. Players need to work on ball control, passing, dribbling and receiving the ball. They also need to develop what's known as team play, or team sense. All of these come from practice and play. There's no other way to get them.

RECEIVING THE BALL

Sooner or later the ball will be aimed right at your child. It may be a light little pass, or it might be a booming shot gone awry. Either way, a decision must be made about what to do with this ball. Ducking is an option, but not one that will increase the player's level of popularity among his teammates. He's not allowed to put his hands up to protect himself either, so what next? Well, the skill is known as receiving the ball, and there are several ways to do that.

BALL CONTROL

The first ball control skill is the simple **trap.** Players have to be able to stop a moving ball, and bring it under control. They do this by absorbing the ball into their bodies, cushioning it so it doesn't bounce off them. The first trap learned is the least painful, and is the foot trap. A ball is pushed (passed) along the ground, and the receiving player tries to control the ball with the feet. There are two ways to do this. The first is by stomping one foot on top of the ball, pinning it between the foot and the ground. Good eye-foot coordination is needed here, and timing is everything. This trap can be effective in a game, but if bungled, the player can look pretty foolish. A more consistent and useful trap involves the turned-out foot, slightly extended in front of the body. As the ball comes into contact with the foot, the leg is drawn back, so that the ball is cushioned, and the momentum is killed.

Other traps

Other body parts can be used to control the ball. The same cushioning motion of the foot trap can be used with the inner fleshy part of the thigh to control bouncing balls, or passes in the air. No one should try to trap a ball with the large muscle at the top of the leg – the quadriceps. It will hurt, and can cause serious bruising.

Keeping the leg turned out, and moving backwards with the ball, will provide a soft place to absorb the ball while affording protection for the large muscles.

If the ball is too high to be trapped with the inner thigh, it may be trapped by the lower abdomen. Use of the stomach muscles is highly recommended, but the same backwards, cushioning motion is needed. The goal is always to bring the ball down to the feet as quickly as possible, and then to play the ball out from under the feet.

9

The ball may also be trapped by the chest. This involves good balance, and following the ball into the body with the eyes. As soon as the ball is going to make contact with the chest, the shoulders should be folded inward so the chest caves in, the head drops, the arms go out and the ball drops to the feet. Another effective chest trap is the opposite of the the first one. This involves sticking the chest out to to meet a high ball, then leaning back to absorb the speed of it. The first style is used when the player meets the ball, or when the ball is coming at her without great velocity and she is closely covered by an opposing player. The second style of trap is the better choice when the ball is coming in at greater speed. The player needs to judge which trap is best at the given moment, and to make that decision early.

The last body part that can be used to control a ball is the head. Unlike the other traps, which involve a cushioning action, heading requires moving toward the ball. Like the other traps, the most important thing for your child is to keep his eyes open and on the ball for as long as possible. The player's weight should start back and swing forward from the hips, keeping the neck rigid so that the player's forehead meets the ball right at the hairline. The ball should be aimed downward to play the ball to oneself, or in the direction of a teammate to make a pass.

The use of the head may sound a little scary, but it really doesn't hurt at all if done properly. The worst thing your child can do is chicken out of heading the ball when it's on its way. Guaranteed nosebleed, face plant or hand ball if he does. Like most soccer skills, determination and confidence go a long way in executing a great play.

When receiving the ball, a player should always be thinking about what she's going to do next. She should always try to screen the ball from her opponents when it comes to her. Then she must decide if she will move away from an attacker with the ball, or control the ball and then pass it, or control it by making a pass. Those really are the three options open, and one of them must be taken. Lastly, it is important in all cases to be moving when receiving the ball. To be stationary is to make oneself into a brick wall. It's much easier to absorb the weight of the ball when moving into its path. Then your child will be deflecting or absorbing its momentum.

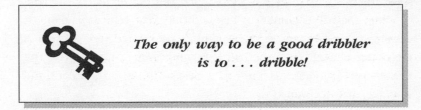

The only way to be a good dribbler is to . . . dribble!

DRIBBLING

Dribbling is the term used to describe moving the ball along the ground with the feet. Players should be able to dribble the ball with the inside and outside of both feet, keeping the head up to see where they are going, and who is coming in to tackle them. Dribbling is used to move the ball up the field, to create scoring opportunities, to evade opposing players and to create time and space to make a pass or take a shot. It is a technique that is never perfected or completely mastered. It takes agility, balance and quick thinking to be a great dribbler. It also means having a good feel for the ball, because players need to be watching where they are going and who is coming to tackle them while they are dribbling, rather than watching their feet and the ball. Experienced dribblers feel like the ball is attached to their feet with a string, and that they can push the ball away and bring it back with ease. Coordinating ball control with speed and the strength to hold off tacklers is the ideal dribbling goal so that the player can hold onto the ball long enough to make a good pass or shot.

Part of dribbling is faking and feinting around other players. This is the part that the hot-doggers love! Coming up with new moves and jazzy fakes to fool the opponent is fun and develops the techniques needed to be a good dribbler. Staying balanced with the weight over the ball and on the balls of the feet is the optimum position for feinting as well as dribbling. When getting ready to feint, players need to keep the ball near them and moving. A dead ball is a sitting duck! They should also keep the feet and body moving too. It's far easier to keep moving than to stop dead and start again.

KICKING

There are many kinds of kicks in soccer. Each of them uses a specific area on the foot, and each has its own type of back swing and follow-through. Kids need to be able to control their kicks so that the ball does what they want it to, and so they avoid unnecessary fouls by kicking out of control.

The first way kids kick the ball is usually the **toe kick**, or **toe hack**. This may be very impressive at first because the ball can go a long way – but it's not a very effective style of kicking because it is very hard to control the direction of the ball off the toe. A good coach will try to eliminate the toe hack very quickly.

A more effective style of kicking for control over the direction is the **push pass**. Using the inside of the foot, with the knee turned out, players push the ball along the ground to each other. This pass is usually short and crisp and very precise. Players should be able to give and receive push passes while on the move.

Another type of pass uses the outside of the foot. It is sometimes referred to as the **flick pass**. Usually done on the run, the player pushes the ball to the side using the ankle and the outside of the foot. It is difficult to get a great deal of strength behind this pass, so the pass will be short, but it's a sneaky and effective way to get around and through the defense.

The other way to kick the ball is to "**use the laces**." Players usually use this technique when shooting on goal or making longer passes. By pointing the toes, getting one's head and knee over the ball and using a high follow-through, players can kick the ball a great distance with both a high level of velocity and accuracy. A variety of different kicks may result from using different amounts of momentum and follow-through when kicking the ball. By throwing the weight back at the follow-through, a good loft can be attained – perfect for passing the ball over opponents' heads, or across the goal mouth for a shot using the head.

A push pass

Little **chip passes** are made by digging the laces under the ball and punching it into the air, using little to no follow-through with the leg. To get more power behind the ball, players need to drive through the middle of the ball, rather than under it, keeping their weight forward and concentrated. Because this type of kick requires balance and timing, it's a good idea to tell players to put their arms out. This aids in the performance of the skill. The other types of passes are more sneaky and subtle. For power, the arms need to go up and forward, so that one strides into the kick.

SHOOTING

All the kicking styles discussed above may be used to shoot on goal. Any manner of getting the ball into the net will result in a goal (except using the hands of course), but the usual way is to take a shot. This means kicking the ball into the net from a spot near the penalty area. The most powerful shot comes from using the laces, with the foot driving through the lower-middle part of the ball. The most difficult skill in soccer is making a powerful, accurate shot with a single touch with the ball in the air (**the volley shot**). The best strikers in the world are able to do it, but not every time! The moral of the story is to keep practicing and developing power and accuracy in shooting and passing. These really are the keys to success for the entire game.

DEFENDING

A soccer game consists of two main phases – attacking and defending. The above skills pertain to the attack. Your child's team has the ball and wishes to maintain control over it. The other part of the game revolves around the other team, and when they control the ball. This is defending. As soon as a team loses control of the ball, no matter where the ball is on the field, the team goes into defense mode. What does this mean? To start it means doing a different sort of mental inventory. Your child will still be looking to see where his teammates are on the field, and where the opposition players are – but rather than looking for open space to play the ball to, or to fill himself, he will be looking to see where the dangerous defensive space is, and checking to see if he or she is goal-side.

> Goal-side means placing oneself between an attacking player and one's own net. When on defense, your child will always want to be goal-side of the player he is marking.

What is dangerous defensive space? It is an area on the playing field from which an opposing team member can score a goal. This space continually changes depending on where the opposing team members are in relation to the ball, where the ball is, and where defenders are in relation to both the ball and the attacking players. If there is an undefended space in front of the goal that an attacking player can get to with ease, that is dangerous defensive space. A defender needs to get goal-side of that space to protect it. A good defender will never let an attacker stand between himself and the net when there is considerable pressure to score. There is always a chance that an attacker will move to an offside position, but it is always a gamble to play that way – one that most coaches won't take. So, defending involves analyzing the field to see where dangerous defensive space is, then moving goal-side to that space so that no attacker has a clear path to the net.

Once in the proper defensive position, the defender must then make another analysis and decision. His goal is to cause the attacking team to lose possession of the ball. There are two ways that can happen. The first way is to stall a shot on net as long as possible and wait for the attacking team to make a mistake. The other way is to force a mistake. And this involves the skill of tackling. There are three elements involved in making a tackle, and they involve knowing when to tackle, where to tackle, and how to tackle. Judging the first two elements is the most important part of the skill.

Several events lead up to a tackle being made. They may occur in lengthy stages, or instantaneously. The first event that must occur is that the defender must be the person closest to the player in possession of the ball. She must then challenge that player. She does that by keeping her body low and her weight forward, between the attacker and the net. When approaching the attacker the player should come in quickly but under control, so that she is approximately three yards away from the ball. She should be watching the ball, using peripheral vision to watch the attacker and other players on the field. The angle of her approaching run will be determined by the position of other defending players and where the out-of-bounds lines are. At all times the defender wants to force the attacking player to the outside, away from the net. She also wants to make sure that she has defensive backup (cover) in case the attacker gets away from her. If she has no cover, then she will be unable to make a tackle. All she will be able to do is jockey for goal-side position with the attacking player, and try to close him down so that he can't make a play. It's important for all players to know that the most dangerous player on the field is the one in possession of the ball. He or she must be covered at all times.

If the defender has someone to cover him, or if there is no other option (because the attacker is speeding in on the goalkeeper, ready to shoot), then she may decide to tackle. She should only make this decision when the attacking player has momentarily lost control of the ball, or when he can get to the ball in one step.

A player may be deemed to have lost control of the ball when he must take a step to control it. This means that as soon as he has touched the ball, he has lost control of it.

Once the defender has decided to seize the opportunity to tackle, she must know how to do it – legally. It's easy to **tackle** illegally: just push the guy onto the ground, or trip him, or otherwise stop him from touching the ball. The legal way to tackle is to use the body and the feet to take possession of the ball. How to do this? Step as close to the ball as possible, then use the other foot to contact the ball. Move into the player's space and contact the ball with both speed and determination, and keep the weight of the body moving through the ball. Keep watching the ball and move immediately after the ball to touch it again to regain possession of it. Be prepared to use one's shoulders to push against the weight of the other player and to shield the ball from him. Try to stay on one's feet and well balanced when tackling. Only desperation tackles, known as **slide tackles**, involve hurling the body at the ball and knocking it out-of-bounds or into neutral territory. The slide tackle is a very special skill that requires more of a hands-on demonstration than can be afforded here, but it involves approaching the attacking player from the side (or alongside), coming in at high speed and sliding in low and across the ball with the foot. The foot nearest the attacker is tucked up and under the body as the tackler slides along the pitch. The position on the ground is similar to that found in hurdle running. The objective is to clear the ball away from the attacker and out of harm's way.

If our stalwart defender is responsible for covering other defending players or dangerous space, she must also keep herself goal-side of other attackers, watching for them to make runs towards the net and into dangerous space. She should try to intercept a pass made to the opposing player if she is in a position to do so. Otherwise she needs to put herself in a position where she can jockey the attacking player and hopefully isolate him so that he can neither pass nor shoot.

ATTACKING

As soon as the defense takes the ball away from the other team, it is on the attack. The transition must be instantaneous – the drive to the goal is on! Rather than marking players on the other team and sticking close to them, teammates try to find empty space where they are open to receive a pass. Everyone will be alert to any opening or opportunity to get the ball upfield and into the other team's goal as quickly as possible. Whoever managed to steal the ball away from the other team will probably try to feed the ball upfield to a forward or to one of the midfielders, who will act as the "quarterback" in setting up the offense.

The players will use a combination of dribbling, kicking, passing and ball control skills to keep the ball away from the other team and work the ball upfield and into dangerous defensive space to create a scoring opportunity. There are several types of offensive strategies, but the two most common are the "kick-and-run" style of play and the multiple-passing, overlapping offense style of play. The first involves trying to spring a forward or two free on a breakaway or to an unguarded space where they can have a free shot on goal. A long, overhead pass and a perfectly timed run are the key ingredients to this style of play. The second style involves making precision passes that are short and sharp and make the defensive players run around so much that they are caught out of position. When that happens, the attacking team sends a player into the unguarded space to receive a pass and take a shot on net.

The systems of play can get very complex, and beyond the scope of this book, but it's enough to understand that children need to work on all their skills to fit both styles of offense into their repertoire. Coaches will choose the system of play that best suits the skill sets of their players. Beyond that, it's up to the players on the field to use their heads to make good decisions about the passes they make. There is always a free-wheeling element to a soccer game. Unlike basketball or volleyball which rely on specific offensive formations and plays, soccer is an organic process where players take advantage of defensive mistakes to move into unguarded space.

Players need to watch each other all the time and tell each other where they are, or where they are going to be, so that they have a number of passing and playmaking options open to them all the time.

When moving to the attack, it is important that defenders support midfielders and midfielders support forwards. This means following behind and alongside the player who is carrying (dribbling) the ball and staying away from players on the other team so that they are available to receive a pass. The objective is to have players ahead of the ball, beside the ball and behind the ball. That way the ball can get knocked away in any direction and a teammate will be there ready to take control of it. Without sufficient support from teammates, a team will lose possession of the ball regularly and be forced into playing defense for the whole game.

COMMUNICATION

Teammates who talk to each other on the field are generally more successful than those who don't. There are several types of talking. One involves team talk, which is general and specific encouragement of teammates. Cheering on the team is a good motivator for everyone involved, and should be encouraged. Later on in your son or daughter's development, more specific talk should be encouraged. Calling for passes and shouting for a player to make a run is very helpful in playmaking. Another very important type of call to make is "man on!" – meaning an opposing player is approaching so do something with the ball quickly. Players should also call the ball when more than one player could receive it.

Players are not allowed to say "mine" or "I've got it" (it's considered poor sportsmanship), so they need to call out their own names or their shirt colors, or something else that identifies them specifically when calling for the ball.

Not all communication is verbal. Players may whistle or use hand or arm signals to call for the ball. They may also work out a numbered code system for types of passes and plays they want to set up. A nod of the head or rolling the eyes in a specific direction tells a teammate where to send the ball next. Teammates need to be encouraged to communicate at all levels, and to do so regularly throughout games and practices. The increase in effective play-making can be very remarkable indeed.

After several years of playing, youngsters should be quite proficient in the skills and team play described above. You should feel free to talk to coaches about skill development and the goals and objectives they have set for your son or daughter. Being aware of where they are on the field, and where others and the ball are, is critical to making intelligent decisions, and the decision to act always comes before the action. A less skilled player who makes good decisions can be much more effective than one who has a terrific shot but who lets it rip at exactly the wrong time. Part of the joy of soccer is in the organic play-making process, and this is the result of the development of good game sense and soccer skills. Much of soccer offense is the result of strong communication, trust and play-making sense among teammates.

Here's what the coaches look for ...

HEADING
a) Eyes open
b) Attack the ball
c) Part of head
d) Meet ball at its highest point
e) One foot take off
f) Direction
(high & wide: defensive/down: attacking)

PASSING
a) Accuracy/eye on the ball
b) Pace/weight/timing
c) Part of foot & ball
d) Decision making

RECEIVING THE BALL
a) Body behind the ball
b) Attack the ball
c) First touch
d) Eye on the ball
e) Head up

DEFENDING
a) Goal side
b) Speed & angle of approach
c) See the ball & player
d) Prevent forward movement
e) Keep balanced
f) Threaten the ball
g) Eye on the ball

DRIBBLING
a) See the ball & player
b) See the player
c) Change of speed/direction
d) Skill
e) Attack the player

SHOOTING
a) Accuracy before power
b) Eye on the ball/head steady
c) Part of foot & ball

SUPPORT
a) Angle of support (front & behind ball)
b) Near, far & wide
c) Communication (verbal & eye contact)
d) Support the player & ball

GOALKEEPING
a) Eye on the ball
b) Body behind the ball
c) Attack the ball
d) Decision making

These are key coaching words which kids will hear at practice.

Courtesy: Jim Cannovan

CHAPTER THREE

The rules spelled out

If your child is going to play any sport, it's a good idea to have an understanding of what is allowed and what is not at any given time on the playing field. There are reasons beyond the obvious ones for this: chiefly, it allows everyone involved to enjoy the game better, it increases player confidence and sportsmanship and it significantly reduces the complaints heaped on game officials. The net effect is a happier team, coach, referee and fans on the sidelines – and happiness is what playing is all about.

OFFICIALS

A soccer game is governed by three officials: the referee and two linesmen (or referee assistants). Unique among competitive sports, the soccer referee has complete control over the game, including how long the game lasts, who may come and go from the field, when a player is fouled and whether to call the foul or not. Everyone must defer to the referee's decisions, and there is very little room for appeal. The referee is considered to be the authority on the field, and can overrule anyone's opinion, including the linesmen's. The chief purpose of the referee is to ensure the game goes along in a safe, timely and orderly manner. In order to do that he or she needs to run along with the play and watch it carefully. When a goal is scored, or a serious infraction occurs, the referee makes a note in his notebook of when the event occurred, who was involved and what happened. That way there is a report to look back on in case of appeal. But generally speaking, the only time the "book" appears is after a goal. The rest of the time it resides in the referee's pocket as he runs around, following the play.

The referee – the authority on the field.

Linesmen are responsible for watching these things – did the ball go out-of-bounds and, if so, who touched it last, and are all players in an on-side position during play? Because the on-side rule is a difficult one, and the call is so controversial, only really good linesmen (accredited) are usually allowed to make that call. Linesmen, too, must run along with the play up and down the sidelines (touch lines) of the field. There are two systems for doing this. One system makes a linesman responsible for running up and down the sideline to the halfway line, and calling offsides on that half of the field only, as well as throw-ins, goal kicks and corner kicks. The other system, which is much more common, is to have the linesman run up and down the entire length of the field, keeping up with the play, and calling offsides, throw-ins and corner and goal kicks at both ends of the field. As a spectator, you need to keep clear of the linesmen, allowing them to have a clear view of the action and a straight run up the sidelines.

During regular season play, most leagues provide a referee, and the two opposing teams are responsible for providing a linesman. When that happens, the referee usually opts to make the offside calls herself.

START OF THE GAME

Possession of the first kickoff is established by a coin toss with the two team captains and the referee at center field. After that, players line up on opposing sides of the halfway line, prepared to do battle. The team that wins the toss must select which end of the field it would prefer to start with, and the loser gets to kick off. To do that a number of players line up along the halfway line, with the ball right at center. The opposing team must stand 10 yards away from the ball, and can only approach the ball after it completely crosses the halfway line. Once the ball is in play (when it is touched and moves forward), the game has begun, and anything can happen from there. The referee checks the time, and keeps track of it from then on. A regulation game is 90 minutes long, consisting of two 45-minute halves, and up to a 15-minute half-time break. There are no time-outs and no stoppages allowed except for injuries. The referee can add time on to the game to make up for time lost during those occasions. Different leagues and different levels of play may have varying lengths of games, so check those details at registration.

THE GAME CONTINUES

Players go about playing the game by passing and dribbling the ball with their feet. The object is to control the ball amongst one's teammates long enough to work it up the field and into the other team's net. Certain obstacles may present themselves on the way, which consist mainly of other players and the touch lines. If the ball is inside the playing field, it is **in play**. Once it crosses any boundary line completely, it is **out** or **gone into touch**, and play stops. If the ball happens to go out on a sideline, there is only one way of getting the ball back into play, and that is called a **throw-in**. The linesman indicates the ball is out by putting his hand straight up. He then indicates which team has possession of the throw-in by pointing with his hand or a flag. The team that touched the ball last before it went over the touch line (sideline) loses possession of the ball, and the other team gets to throw the ball in. If a player doesn't get the throw right in a game, the ball is turned over to the other team, and one of its member gets to attempt a throw. Once someone gets it right and the ball is touched by another player, it is considered back in play, and the game continues.

There is a specific technique to throwing the ball in. It must be thrown with both hands overhead. Both feet must remain on the ground and the ball must be released from the hands as it reaches the area above the forehead. This is probably the single most flubbed skill in the early years of soccer playing, and requires a great deal of practice to get right.

FREE KICKS

If the ball goes out-of-bounds across the end or goal line, one of two things may happen, depending on which team touched the ball last. If an **offensive player** kicks the ball out over the end line, the defensive team gets possession of the ball and is allowed to take a **goal kick**. This is a re-start or set play where the ball is placed anywhere on the six-yard line and kicked in to the field. The ball must travel outside the 18-yard box, and be touched by another player to be considered back in play. Goal kicks can get a little tricky, especially when dealing with little tikes who have trouble kicking a ball all that way, but it makes the game more exciting for the fans, and that's what the FIFA rules are all about. Once the ball is back in play, the game continues.

If the ball leaves the playing field across the goal line and a **defensive player** was the last one to touch it, a whole new play develops, called the **corner kick**. The ball must sit within the quarter circle arc and be passed to another player or kicked into the goal. A goal may be scored directly from the kick. The corner kick is a type of set play that can get very complicated in terms of strategy and play-making and adds greatly to the excitement of the game.

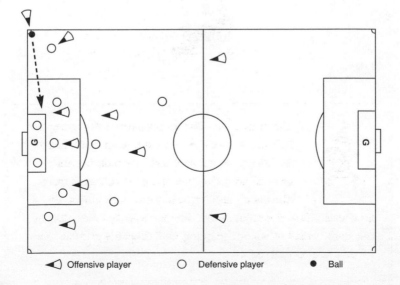

◁ Offensive player   ○ Defensive player   ● Ball

FOULS AND PENALTIES

In the perfect soccer game, throw-ins, goal kicks, corner kicks and goals would be the only stoppages in play. In the perfect soccer game everyone would go home very happy and smug that such a clean and skilful game had been played. However, it is unlikely that any such game has been played in the history of soccer, and never will be in a kids' match. As a result there are a number of other rules pertaining to fouls and penalties that must also be addressed.

Soccer is a very physical sport with lots of bodily contact. That bodily contact is commonly known as a **tackle**. A legal tackle occurs when a player approaches an opposing player who has possession of the ball, and manages to take the ball away without fouling that player. One may only tackle from the front or the side of the player in possession of the ball. Furthermore, one may only tackle by playing the ball with the feet. The number one criterion is that a player must *play the ball*, not the other player. Having said that, it's perfectly legal to apply a little pressure on opposing players by using the side of the body to gain an advantageous position on the ball. One can swoop in from the side and sort of lean up against the player being tackled and try to take the ball away. Once anything other than the shoulder gets involved, it becomes an illegal tackle and the referee should stop the game for a **free kick**.

Using the hands in any way is a major no-no in soccer. No pushing, grabbing, holding someone at bay, tickling, pointing, poking or touching with the hands is permitted. This pertains to the ball while it's in play, as well as opposing players.

There are two types of free kicks – direct and indirect. The **direct free kick** is awarded when a player kicks, attempts to kick, trips, jumps at, charges, strikes, pushes, holds or spits at an opponent, or deliberately uses the hand or arm to control the ball. The referee indicates a direct free kick by using a hand signal after he points to the spot the kick is to be taken from. In a recent rule change, kickoff and goal kicks are also considered direct kicks, in addition to corner kicks, which means a goal may be scored from them. The **indirect free kick** results from dangerous play, charging unfairly when the ball isn't being played, impeding another player's progress and charging the goalkeeper in the goal area. An offside call, playing a free kick or throw-in to oneself, the cautioning of a player and the illegal handling of the ball by the goalkeeper inside the goal area also result in indirect free kicks. This means the ball must be touched by another player before a goal may be scored. The referee indicates an indirect kick by keeping his arm straight in the air until the ball is kicked. There are a number of strategies and set plays that revolve around free kicks and they are a very exciting part of the game.

If an infraction takes place in the penalty area, and the offensive team commits the foul, the ball may be placed anywhere in the penalty area to be kicked. If the defensive team commits the foul in the penalty area, the ball must be placed on the 18-yard line perpendicular to where the foul occurred. Everywhere else on the field the ball is kicked from where the foul occurred.

It was pointed out earlier that the referee has complete control over the game. Nowhere is that control more evident than at the time of a foul or infraction. In soccer, there is a **play-on rule**, which goes like this: if a player is fouled during the course of play, but if it would be more disadvantageous to call the foul and stop the play than to let the play carry on, the referee may decide to let the play carry on. The foul is noted, as the referee calls out, "Play on!" (or may indicate this with a sweeping motion of his arms), and the offending player may be spoken to afterward, but the play is permitted to develop. This rule keeps the flow of the game paramount in the players' and fans' minds, and helps to prevent opposing teams from fouling on purpose in order to mess up a perfect breakaway or other fabulous scoring opportunity. If the tackle made is a major foul, the referee will usually make the call and may very well "card" the player for his trouble.

THE CARDS

The referee carries two colored cards, a red one and a yellow one. They are used as a form of discipline on the field, and are reserved for players who foul in a deliberate or unsporting manner. Minor infractions can occur during the course of play where a player really is playing the ball, and gets tangled up with an opposing player. In that situation, it is unlikely that player will be carded. However, if she is involved in a number of minor infractions, the referee will look upon her a little differently. Most likely the referee will issue a verbal warning about the level of play, and that will be the end of it. It's very important that young players learn the values of the game, and that begins with the cardinal rule of playing the ball at all times, and not the other player. If she keeps this idea at the fore at all times, she won't get into foul trouble. Sometimes, though, a single foul is severe enough on its own to merit a card, and the rules are very specific about which fouls merit which cards.

Yellow card fouls

- unsporting behavior
- failing to give 10 yards at free kicks
- delaying the restart of play
- entering the field without permission
- persistently breaking the rules
- dissenting with the referee

Red card fouls

- violent conduct
- serious foul play
- using offensive, insulting or abusive language
- using the hands to prevent a goal from scoring

It's very difficult to watch a youngster make a deliberate foul. A child who makes a malicious tackle or loses his temper on the field needs to be dealt with immediately and in a serious manner. It is not the referee's job to do so, but he will if the coach does not remove the child from the game. It may appear that the referee is being more lenient, but there is a greater level of tolerance for mistakes when children are learning the game. So, there is room for some cooperation between the coach and the referee in the early years of playing. Once a child is older, he will be held responsible for his own bad decisions and be subjected to the disciplinary measures associated with being carded.

In the event a card is issued, the offending player is called aside by the referee and is formally shown the yellow card. Then his or name is written down in the referee's notebook, along with the team name, the player's number and the infraction. The yellow card is a formal caution, and it means that the player is considered a menace to others, and any other bad play or questionable conduct will not be tolerated. If presented with a second yellow card, the referee will then show the player the red card, which means he has been ejected from the game. The player must leave, and the team must play shorthanded for the rest of the game.

Major fouls of a malicious nature may earn a player a red card right away. Soccer is a tough physical game, but there is little or no tolerance for nastiness and lack of sportsmanship at any age or skill level.

HAND BALL

One of the most serious infractions in soccer is the hand ball. Players are not allowed to play the ball with their arms or hands. This means they can't bat the ball, punch the ball, swat at the ball, or touch the ball in any way that alters the direction or speed of the ball. There is such a thing as the ball hitting a player's arm accidentally, which is allowable, but a player is responsible for keeping the arms under control. Making a call, or not, is at the referee's discretion.

If a defensive player uses his *hands* within the penalty area (the goal area), the penalty is very severe. The opposing team is awarded a **penalty kick**. If the ball is on its way into the net, and a player other than the goalkeeper prevents a goal from being scored by using his hands, he receives an automatic red card. It used to be considered a savvy defensive play to stop the ball from crossing the goal line any way one could, the thinking being that it was better to take a chance on a penalty shot than to give up a sure goal. The new rule that makes such a play a red card offense has changed people's thinking considerably. Similarly, any player who deliberately interferes with play with the hands on the rest of the playing field may find himself being dealt with just as harshly by the referee. The moral of the story is for your child to think long and hard before moving the hands or the arms one hair towards the ball in a soccer game.

OFFSIDE

There is one last rule regarding play that is complicated to explain, and even trickier to call on the field, and that is offside. The rule states that **there must be two defending players between or level with an offensive player and the goal line when a forward pass is made**. This basically means that offensive players cannot hang out in the other team's half, waiting for the ball to be passed to them. They must run out of the other team's half when they lose possession of the ball to the defending team – or at least back to the level of the last person back. The goalkeeper may be included as one of the defensive players, so there needs to be one defender between an offensive player and the net at the time a pass is made.

When a player is offside, and a forward pass is made to her, the linesman will put up his flag, and the referee will blow the whistle to stop play. The referee must let a play develop, because there is no offside until a pass is made. If the player carrying the ball elects to shoot instead, the player in the offside position is irrelevant, unless she is blocking the goalkeeper's view of the shot or impeding his ability to make the save. If the shot rebounds off the goalkeeper or the goalpost, and the player that was in the offside position gets the rebound and scores, the goal doesn't count. (The following diagrams illustrate some common offside dilemmas.) Lastly, a player may be in an offside position as a forward pass is made, but if he's running away from the play, back up the field, offside will not be called.

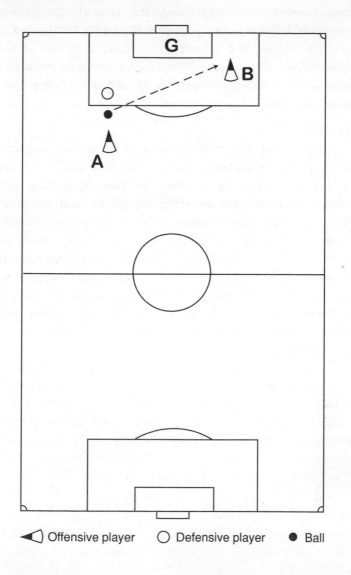

◁◗ Offensive player   ○ Defensive player   ● Ball

Offside: B is offside at the moment the ball is passed because there is only one defender (the goalkeeper) between B and the goal. (Other players are not shown in this diagram.)

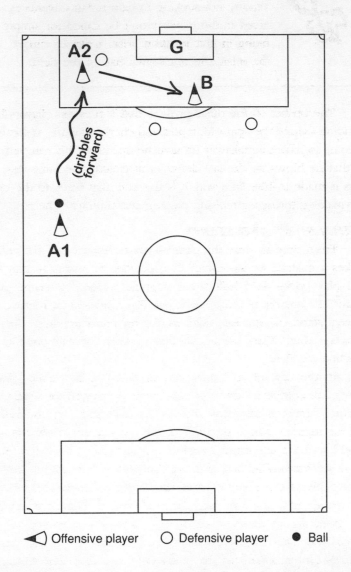

◀ Offensive player   ○ Defensive player   ● Ball

*Offside: B is **not** offside because at the moment A passes the ball there are two defensive players between B and the goal. This is true even if the defenders are not in an immediate position to stop a shot by B.*

> If a player is in an offside position but *clearly* not seeking to gain unfair advantage from it, the player won't be called for simply being in that position. Also, a player cannot be offside in one's own half of the field.

The upshot of the offside rule is that it prevents players from standing around the opposition goal and cherry picking. If someone is going to have a breakaway on goal, he must time his run perfectly so that he blows by the last defender at exactly the same time the pass is made to him. In a way it is this rule that leads to the crafty playmaking, through precision passing and timing of the run.

OTHER STOPS AND STARTS

From time to time the game stops for injuries, or the referee makes a mistake, or someone's dog decides he wants to play too, and play grinds to a halt. What happens to get the game going again? The answer is a drop ball. Just like a face-off in hockey, two players stand on opposite sides of the referee, who drops the ball between them. They aren't allowed to kick the ball until it has touched the field.

In the case of an injury and no foul has happened, play is allowed to continue. Only when the game is stopped for some other reason is medical attention allowed on the field. In the case of serious injuries (and a scrape may be considered serious at your child's level), a teammate or even an opposing player may show good sportsmanship and put the ball out-of-bounds so that the injured player can receive assistance. At the younger levels of play the referee may not wait very long, or even at all, before stopping the game for an injury, even though she's not supposed to. She should wait until the ball is in fairly neutral territory so that neither team is too punished by the position of the drop ball. Once the player has been looked at and cannot continue playing, he must leave the field quickly so that play can carry on. It seems harsh, but remember that all the rules have been developed out of World Cup competition, where all sorts of tricks and grandstanding have been known to happen.

Other things to watch out for include improperly taken free kicks and infractions surrounding the goalkeeper. Free kicks in beehive soccer can get confusing, and in the melee the kicker may try to kick the ball twice (before someone else has a chance to touch it). That's a no-no, and the referee has to give a free kick from the same spot to the other team.

CHAPTER FOUR

Variations on the game

MINI-SOCCER

Ninety percent of what players do in a soccer game revolves around what happens when they don't have the ball. This being the case it becomes important to teach children what to do when they don't have the ball. This involves using the space around them to develop playmaking strategies. The 11 per side, 90-minute game involves a great many people running around a vast space not touching the ball very much. For the youngest players a regulation-size field is impossible to deal with. Furthermore, the whole idea of developing ball control, passing and kicking skills is lost because they just don't get the opportunity to do those things that often. Hence the mini-soccer game for younger players was born.

In mini-soccer, children are exposed to the frequent repetition of skills in small game situations, which allows young tikes to have a few specific opportunities to pass, and a higher percentage of touches. The game uses the width of a regulation field as the length, and has a smaller goal area and net. The mini-goal is four-feet high and 10-feet wide, as opposed to the eight-foot-high and 24-foot-wide adult goal. The diagram below shows how a regulation-size field is adapted to become two mini-soccer fields.

In mini-soccer, five to seven players plus a goalkeeper play per side, and there are frequent substitutions. There is no offside rule, but no one may score from within the eight-yard arc (which is the mini-soccer penalty area). This way the little tikes get much more exposure to the ball and have fewer targets to pass to, lessening confusion and panic, and encouraging greater team-work and

35

organization. There is still a beehive, but it turns out to be much smaller. Skills are introduced gradually, and the emphasis is on having fun and kids developing at their own rates. The kids who are on the field are all able to concentrate on the game because there's a much greater chance they may actually touch the ball.

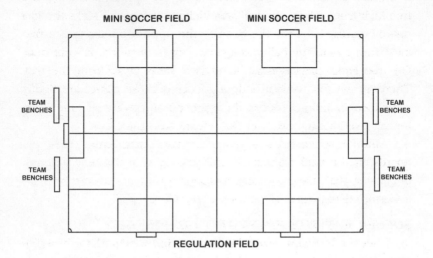

INDOOR SOCCER

People who play soccer outdoors run the risk of becoming addicted to the game, and rather than turn to basketball, volleyball or cross-country skiing when it gets too cold, they try to find an indoor venue to get their fix. Fortunately a number of arenas have been converted in recent years to indoor soccer fields. Even if there isn't one in your area, a gym makes a fine substitute.

Indoor soccer is comparable to ice hockey. The game is played with five players and a goalkeeper on each side, and play is continuous for 20 minutes. Substitutions are done on the fly, as in hockey, and players can be thrown into the penalty box for deliberate fouls or unsportsmanlike conduct. It is a fast-paced game, with many short passes and lots of ball control. The equipment is the same as outdoor soccer, and so are the rules in terms of fouls, but there are a number of additional rules that help to keep the play moving and the ball under control.

Like a hockey rink, the field is divided into three zones. Players can't be offside in indoor soccer, but the ball cannot be passed over three lines. This prevents players from blasting the ball from one end of the field to the other, and forces them into crafty playmaking. If the ball is passed forward three lines, the opposing team gets a free kick from where the ball was kicked. If a player kicks the ball out-of-bounds (i.e., over the boards), the opposing team gets a free kick from where the ball was kicked (not from where it went out). On free kicks players must stand two yards away from the ball. There are no throw-ins in indoor soccer. Because games are tightly scheduled in indoor soccer, there are no stoppages in time. Only for very serious injuries will the referee stop the clock.

Indoor soccer is a fast-paced and exciting game. Using the boards, or the wall, to make a wall pass, gives it a whole different dimension that doesn't exist in outdoor soccer. For soccer nuts, it's a toss-up as to which game they enjoy more!

SOCCER FOR THE PHYSICALLY CHALLENGED

Soccer is highly adaptable for the indoors, and for children with varying degrees of physical mobility. It affords flexibility in terms of both gross and fine motor skills, and can be played even by those using motorized wheelchairs.

The motor soccer game may be structured as follows: athletes assemble on a regulation basketball court. Five players and a goalkeeper aside is preferable, and substitutions should be made freely, like indoor soccer. At either end of the court there should be a defined goal area, with a line on the floor established as "the goal." The goal could be as large as the width of the gymnasium to a metre or two wide, depending on the skill level of the players. The object is to push or shoot the ball over the opponent's goal line with the wheelchair.

The game runs like a regulation indoor soccer game, with two 30-minute halves and a five or 10-minute half-time. There is no out-of-bounds, so play is continuous. The goal area should be of a reasonable space, and if a foul occurs within it a penalty shot can be taken. There should be a two-metre distance between all other players and the ball on the goal line, with only a designated goalkeeper between the "kicker" and the net. When the referee blows the whistle, the kicker can attempt to score by taking a shot, one-on-one.

Equipment revolves around safety, and should include a rubber bumper box fitted into the footrests at the front of the wheelchair, and padding to protect players' feet and shins. The ball should be large enough that it doesn't get trapped under the carriage of the wheelchair and bouncy enough that passes can be made. A coach may need to experiment with a number of different types of balls to find the right one.

CHAPTER FIVE

Now your child is in a league

SIGNING UP

The best source of information on signing up your child in a league is the local or community newspaper. Start looking in late January or early February for ads indicating the name of the league, where and when to sign up and any additional information. You can try the library and town or city hall for information as well. Local sporting goods stores, particularly shops specializing in soccer equipment and uniforms, will also have information about leagues in your area. The provincial soccer association or the Canadian Soccer Association will be able to provide you with the names of leagues or clubs, both outdoor and indoor, near you. The address is located in Chapter 10, Sportsmania.

At registration you will be asked to fill out a registration form. On it you will be asked your child's birth date, address, the number of years she has played soccer, and to indicate her playing ability (beginner, average, above average). You will also be asked if you are willing to volunteer to help out. Before ignoring this question, consider that the league is almost entirely made up of volunteers and wouldn't exist without people like you giving a bit of their time. There are many ways in which parents can help out. Registration is the perfect time to find out what they are.

One word of advice is to get to registration on time. Leagues can fill up fast, and late sign-ups can be difficult, if not impossible. The people who run the leagues are highly committed to the game and expect the players and parents to be the same. It's not a good sign if you can't get your child to registration on time.

AGE GROUPINGS

Soccer leagues categorize teams by age based on year of birth, then gender. The youngest players are usually five or six, and they start with mini-soccer. At this stage teams are composed of both boys and girls, since there are few differences between them. Once they get beyond mini-soccer, they will usually start playing in same-gender leagues.

In highly organized communities with a high demand for soccer, parents may be able to choose to keep their children in mini-soccer, or to have them play on a regulation-size field in a more competitive environment at around the age of nine. Teams are put together based on age, then geography. Soccer is so popular that there is usually a league for every birth year. Leagues are titled under-seven, under-eight, under-nine, etc., up to under-21, then over-21 or adult leagues. In smaller communities several age groups may be combined. Geographically speaking, every team needs a home field, and the league organizers will try to put a team together that can easily get to one central field.

Ability is not a factor in house-league soccer. Soccer club conveners gather all the names after registration and place them on team rosters along with a coach. They will try to balance the teams in terms of the ability and experience ratings parents provided on the registration forms, but by and large it's a completely egalitarian process. The club or league organizers will look for sponsors to cover some or all of the cost of the uniforms. For the sponsors it's a great way to create goodwill in the community (also it's a tax write-off) and makes it easy to come up with a team name! Once the kids are signed up and put on a team, everyone just has to wait patiently for the snow to melt.

Tryouts for representative or club teams are held in the springtime and it appears that there are competitive teams in virtually every age group in every large community in Canada. In representative soccer, there is a team for every birth year, starting with under-11-year-old girls and under-9-year-old boys all the way up to 19-year-olds and over. These teams compete in various regional leagues around the province, and then may vie against one another for the provincial and national championships. Each team will try to find a sponsor, or several sponsors, to help cover the costs of travel and tournaments associated with playing at that level.

LEAGUE ETIQUETTE

At registration you will be informed about game times and when you will contacted with a schedule, home field location, team roster and the time and place of the first team meeting with the coach. What you may or may not be told about are the smaller rules associated with being a soccer mom or dad that come under the umbrella of etiquette.

The date of the first game is mainly determined by the weather. If the fields are going to last the summer, then they must be looked after over the winter, and even more importantly left alone in the early spring so that they can firm up and have grass firmly rooted in them. If the league managers ask teams to stay off the fields until a specific date, it's vitally important to do so. Once a field becomes a dust bowl, it's ruined for life. Communities just don't have the resources to pay for re-sodding or seeding every year.

As soon as the magic date has passed, there is some organizational work to do. At the team meeting, try to establish a logistical arrangement with other parents about transportation to both home and away games. Carpooling to games and practices is a good idea. Don't be shy about sharing these duties with other parents. Talk about a driving and supervising schedule. Most likely you will want to get to know the other parents at the first games and practices. You will probably want to be at all of the games as well, but in case you can't make it it's good to have some backup. Just remember that carpooling and taking turns watching games and practices means just that – taking turns. If you don't feel that you are able to share in those responsibilities with other parents, then it's probably best to stay out of a cooperative arrangement with them.

At the games and practices, it's best to let the coach handle the coaching duties. Talking to your child in the middle of a practice will distract him from what the coach is teaching him. Remember, in the early years especially, fun is the number one priority, with skill development and learning the game falling second and third. Try not to pressure your child to perform. Be positive and supportive, and develop a team ethic yourself. Being overly critical can be damaging to both individual and team confidence. It is exactly contrary to the values that the coach and league are trying to instill in your child. So, if you feel the urge to criticize anyone or anything, bite your tongue, and find a way to turn a negative into a positive.

Help your child to prepare for the game mentally and logistically. If time is a pressure, encourage your child to have her gym bag all packed and ready to go early in the day. Have uniforms washed and ready in the same place every time so there is no last-minute panic. If long hair is an issue, have hair elastics handy with the uniform. Try to keep the home environment calm and organized to combat the butterflies that are going strong in your child's stomach. If she doesn't feel like eating a whole lot for dinner, the butterflies are probably why.

Sometimes just getting out the door can be a grind, if not a finely organized military mission. Knowing this in advance and planning for it will definitely help. The better prepared you are, the more relaxed your child will be, which will help him to focus on the game. Try not to grill him on the game, or skills, or any specifics. This puts undo pressure on the child. Save a mini coaching session for a time in between practices and games. The goal is to have fun – remember!

At the game the kids will be very aware that you are watching. If you've been able to let the coach handle the kids at practice, they should be less likely to try to put on a show for you, but there is still going to be some performance anxiety. You need to find a way to cheer your child on enthusiastically without being a complete distraction. Don't run up and down the field with your child, yelling the entire time. Have faith in his ability to make good decisions. Maintain a good sense of humor and empathy, and encourage good play, good sportsmanship and a go-for-goal attitude throughout the game. Everything you say will have an impact on how your child feels about himself, his teammates, officials, coaches and other fans and parents. You need to role-model the type of treatment you would expect from your child towards all of those people. If a specific concern arises with any of those people, you need to address it in a private moment. During a game you need to defer to the coach and the referee's decisions.

Sportsmanship is another value that is developed in soccer. Unsporting conduct is an infraction of the rules, and is punishable by ejection from the game. Every league has its own rules about how to deal with players who have been unsportsmanlike and red-carded, but they are usually suspended from play for one additional game and given a reprimand from league officials. Repeat offenders are thrown out of the league. There really is no tolerance for players who don't respect others and the rules of the game. Soccer inculcates those values in a number of unofficial ways. Not only must soccer players play within the rules, but they must follow unofficial protocol to demonstrate their sportsmanship. For instance, players must stand 10 yards away from a ball that has been placed for a free kick. Players who violate this rule may be yellow-carded for unsporting conduct. Furthermore, any player who is in the process of being carded must stand a respectful distance away from the referee, and receive any sort of speech the referee feels like delivering, until he is dismissed. If he doesn't, he may be red-carded, and that's the end of his day.

Players show their sportsmanship on the field by helping each other up if they've fallen during play, regardless of which team they are on; by apologizing and shaking hands after an infraction; by running to get a ball that has gone out-of-bounds rather than walking. Some leagues allow player substitutions on throw-ins. It is considered unsportsmanlike to substitute only on the other team's throw, in an attempt to slow the game down. Most referees catch on to this ploy and give the coach what-for, but it doesn't prevent many of them from trying it.

Part of proper league etiquette involves encouraging good sportsmanship, and the most important part of learning good sportsmanship is learning how to be a gracious loser. It may be very upsetting to lose, and players may get angry, or cry, when it happens. But the harsh reality is, there must be a winner and there must be a loser at the end of the day. Players must show their recognition and acceptance of this fact, by shaking hands with opposing team players after games. At the very least, team captains should shake hands at the coin toss prior to a game. Being a good loser means putting one's feelings about the loss aside to publicly recognize the good play of the opposition. Kids should be encouraged to give three cheers to the winner after the game, and to cheer them well. It's very sporting, and if there's a "na, na, na, na, na" attitude on the winning team, that cheer will wilt it in short order – it's a very classy move indeed.

If your child is upset and disappointed as a result of losing, be a good listener. Ask her about her feelings and what happened to cause them. Encourage her to talk about her feelings, and get them out. Then turn the discussion towards solutions to problems, and reinforce the idea that everybody gets better by practicing and working hard. Be positive and confident about your child's abilities and don't allow her to give up. If her feelings spill over into game time, allow the coach to handle any problem behavior. Sometimes it's necessary to sit on the bench for a double shift in order to compose oneself. Kids are usually able to bounce back fairly quickly. Once they become teenagers and winning becomes more important, attitude adjustment can become more complex and take longer to accomplish. Learning to deal with frustration and disappointment at an early age will help later on.

Children who are moving well and enjoying playing the game are naturally good sports. It's when they get frustrated, injured, or are sitting on the bench too long that the outlook can sour. It's important for parents to help keep the entire team happy and the mood light during games and practices, and to encourage kids to lighten up when they start to get down. Like anything else, having a good sense of humor makes any activity that much better.

DEALING WITH WEATHER

Soccer is one of the few games that is played in all kinds of weather over a range of field conditions. The following section deals with specific playing conditions and precautions players can take to make playing as comfortable and strategically sound as possible.

In the heat

Most soccer seasons in Canada take place over the summer months. Where there is dry heat, it is absolutely critical that players stay hydrated. This means water, and lots of it. It's important that you make sure your son or daughter takes in sufficient amounts of water prior to game and practice days. The recommended daily intake is six to eight eight-ounce glasses of water per day. If exercising, this amount needs to increase.

Medical experts say that there is no substitute for water to hydrate the human body. The only drinks that come close to it are the sport drinks that are widely available in retail stores. These provide additional salts and sugars (known as electrolytes) that excessive perspiration and muscle fatigue deplete from the body. Natural fruit juices are good for a quick sugar infusion, but they are not effective hydrators. Nor are soft drinks of any type. So, it's best to stick with plain old H_2O, as many times a day as can be managed.

What this means is monitoring what your child drinks and when she drinks it. While watching for water intake, it is probably also a good idea to watch for caffeine and sugar intake as well. It's important for players to be well rested prior to games and practices, and with caffeine-interrupted sleep it's unlikely that kids will be at their athletic best the next day.

When kids are well hydrated prior to game time, they will require less water during the game. However, it is important to have lots of water available at games, both for drinking and for sponging off. A blast of cool water on the temples, face and back of the neck provides a great deal of refreshment.

Glugging down huge slugs of water at half-time can lead to sluggishness and stomach cramps, and should be avoided. Small sips of water at regular intervals throughout the game will keep fluid levels up in the body.

Other performance and health precautions include staying out of the sun and eating healthy food in small amounts throughout the day. A particular risk during tournaments, when kids are outside and unprotected all day, is sun overexposure and heat stroke. Heat stroke is a risk when people are dehydrated and their bodies become overheated. Faintness, dizziness, even blackouts can result. The best prevention for heat stroke is to stay in the shade, stay rested and hydrated. At the very least, kids need to wear sun protection while they are outside. There are a number of sport sunscreens that are perspiration-proof and waterproof. Be sure to equip your child with his own tube, and make sure he wears it! Another risk of excessive sun exposure isn't as serious as heat stroke, but it can sure put a damper on the day, and that is fatigue. Sitting in the sun saps the muscles of energy and makes the body tired. To sum up, to be mentally and physically ready to play a good game of soccer one must be well hydrated, well rested and full of energy, and to do this means to drink, eat and stay out of the heat!

In the cold

FIFA rules don't allow soccer players to wear long pants during a game, with the exception of the goalkeeper. What kids can do in the colder months is wear thermal shorts, or spandex shorts, under their uniforms. The rules state that their shorts must be the same color as their regulation shorts, and approximately the same length. Kids may also wear thermals under their shirts. It is highly recommended that athletes wear warm clothes while warming up, and keep them on until the opening whistle. They should always be worn while sitting on the sidelines. Warm-up exercises need to be done slowly and cautiously, waiting until the muscles are fully warm before doing any stretching.

In the wet

If you plan to be a die-hard soccer fan, you need to plan ahead for your own comfort in the rain. Umbrellas are absolutely mandatory, as well as insulated rubber boots. Without those two items, there can be nothing more miserable for mom and dad than standing in the pouring rain for 95 minutes. If you really can't take it and find yourself volunteering to go get donuts and coffee for everybody, don't feel bad. You can take comfort in knowing that your child is probably having the time of his life!

As long as the ball is waterproof, soccer in the rain can be an absolute riot! Nothing works the way it is supposed to – the ball doesn't bounce, or it picks up speed as it skids off the grass, or stops dead; it's impossible to get a firm footing, and there's lots of slipping and sliding around. Mud splats up into players' faces, getting in their teeth and eyes. Water dripping from the hair can also hamper visibility, which makes it all the more fun. In serious games, kids can find the wet frustrating, so be prepared for some testiness. After all, part of the game is knowing or predicting what will happen next. The rain makes that very difficult to do. The best way to overcome it is for the coach to encourage a high level of communication on the field, and encourage players to shorten passes to control the ball on the ground as much as possible.

 Apples are considered healthy food, but they are not good to eat before or during athletic events. They are hard to digest and can cause gas and cramps. Kids shouldn't eat much during a game; bananas are easily digestible, as are orange slices at half-time. Leave at least an hour between eating dinner and going out to play a game or practice.

Canceling a game

There are only two reasons for a referee to call off a game – fog and lightning. Safety is the main issue, and the referee will keep a careful eye on the conditions. In the case of suspending a game midway through, if several minutes of the second half have passed, the score will stand as it is. If only the first half has been played, then the game is declared suspended and will need to be replayed.

THE PLAYOFFS

During the regular season, teams will face each other a number of times and be given a placing based on the number of points they accumulate. Each league may do it a bit differently, but usually teams get two points for a win, one point for a tie and zero for a loss. In the case of a tie in the standings, the league will usually look at the number of goals the teams scored and subtract the number of goals scored against them, and whoever has the higher number is the higher-ranked team. If it's still a tie, then the league goes by the number of goals scored alone. If the number is exactly the same at the end of the season, then there may be a playoff game, or a coin toss between the coaches to determine the teams' standings. This process may seem exhaustive and somewhat silly, but at the end of the season when only eight teams make it to the playoffs and there are 12 or so teams in the league, it can make a big difference to how long and successful your youngster's season is.

Overtime

Once a team makes it to the playoffs, the rules change a little bit. Tie results are no longer an acceptable outcome, so teams need a way to settle them. Lo and behold, overtime comes into effect. Once the 90 minutes are up and the teams are tied, there is a five-minute break, and the game goes into a 20-minute overtime game. There is a coin toss to decide which side each team will restart on, just like the toss at the start of the game. After 10 minutes, the game is stopped and the teams switch sides. There is no sudden death if a goal is scored during the 20-minute overtime period. The game goes on until the 20 minutes is up. If the game is still a tie, then it's real stress time: penalty kicks.

Penalty kicks

At no time is a single skill and psychological preparation more necessary in soccer than in the taking of penalty kicks. This is true during penalty kicks in a regulation game, but more universally true at the end of a playoff game that has yet to be settled. It is possible that every person left on the field may end up taking a penalty shot, and each of them had better be prepared to score!

Once overtime has been completed, the referee indicates that penalty kicks will commence. This means that the game stops, and no other players can be substituted from that moment on (unless the goalkeeper gets hurt). The players on the field must remain on the field, and those off the field must stay there. The coach is permitted onto the field to organize the players who will be taking the kicks.

A new coin toss takes place to determine which team will kick first. The referee decides which goal will be used to shoot at, and all the players must gather in the center circle. The two goalkeepers are taken down field to the goal area, where they prepare to do battle. The goalkeeper who is being shot at first positions herself on the goal line in the goal. The opposing goalkeeper must stand (or sit) outside the penalty area, at the 18-yard line. The referee places the ball on the penalty spot and summons the first kicker. He notes the kicker's team and number, then stands off to the side and blows his whistle. The kicker then takes the penalty shot. If he scores, it's a goal! If the goalkeeper stops it, or the ball hits the post, the ball is dead, and it's no goal. There are no live rebounds in overtime penalty shots.

The goalkeepers then change positions and the first kicker for the opposing team approaches the penalty spot. The same routine prevails for five kickers from each team. Whoever scores the most goals at the end of the five kicks is the winner. If one team scores more goals than the other team can before its five kicks are up, the kicks will stop and the high scorer declared the winner. If both teams take their five kicks and the game is still tied, the players who have not kicked yet alternate shots until one team has one goal more than the other. This second round of shots is more nerve-wracking than the first because they truly are sudden-death shots. If the team that kicks first scores first in this second round, the player from the opposing team must score for the kicks to continue. If she doesn't, the game is over and her team loses. Someone on the field is bound to have a meltdown before everyone takes a shot and evens up the score, but if that doesn't happen for some bizarre reason, then players carry on with a second shot until there is a winner, or until the sun goes down and it's too dark to continue. If that happens, the game is decided by the drawing of lots or a coin toss by candlelight, then it's good night, ladies!

This format prevails in all playoff action, be it a tournament or the playoffs at the end of the season. At the end of it all (except for mini-soccer), there is a winner and a loser. Of course the best way to win is during game time, but it's just not always possible. Besides, the hot-doggers love the penalty shots. It's a great way to show off (until they miss)!

SO YOU WANT TO COACH?

When kids first get started playing soccer they usually play at school, then sign up with the local community league. In either setting your child's play depends on volunteer coaches and organizers, and those thoughtful people may come looking for you any season now. Deciding to coach a team is a big decision that shouldn't be taken too lightly, nor made with grave reservations. It can be a highly rewarding and fulfilling experience, not to mention a ton of fun. But it does take a little preparation, organization and knowledge.

There are a number of issues to settle before you volunteer. Do a little self-analysis about your own soccer skills and knowledge, your attitudes towards children and having to deal with their parents, and how much free time you have. What are your attitudes towards girls versus boys? Do you prefer teenagers to youngsters? Are you prepared to teach the basics of the game, or do you consider yourself an "elite" coach? Are you a good organizer, with access to photocopiers, a telephone and other support systems? Are you a good communicator – both speaker and listener? Are you a fair person? What is your philosophy behind coaching? Should everyone receive equal game time, regardless of ability? Is being part of a team the most important thing, or is winning games? Despite what you may think, it's necessary to prioritize what your goals are for yourself, the team and your little one.

Speaking of the little one, you need to decide if you are going to coach your child's team, or someone else's. There are pros and cons to coaching your own child – do up a list of each for yourself. It can be a great way to spend more time together, but are you sure this is the venue you want to do that in? As a coach you take on a role entirely different from parent, which may lead you to reveal a whole other side of your personality. You may just discover you are much more competitive than you thought you were, or that you can yell louder than you ever thought possible, or that you can get really crabby in a hurry, and have trouble getting out of it. Coaching tests you on a whole range of levels – let's face it, if it were easy, everyone would be doing it.

CHAPTER SIX

Equipment

One possible reason why soccer has surpassed all other sports in terms of participation is that the equipment needs are few, and this makes the sport incredibly easy on the pocketbook. There really are only two pieces of equipment that soccer players are required to have - shoes and shin pads. The league usually takes care of uniforms (paid by your fees) and other odds and ends such as water bottles, balls, corner flags and nets for the goal.

The most critical piece of equipment after the uniform is a pair of soccer shoes. Soccer shoes are made of vinyl or leather and have short, stubby cleats made of rubber on the soles. There are a number of variations in terms of cleat arrangements, and any pattern is fine, as long as the cleats are round in shape. Some shoes have screw-in cleats that can be changed according to the condition of the field, but usually the molded soles are just fine. It is highly recommended that you get the best pair of shoes in terms of comfort and fit that your budget can justify. There's nothing more frustrating and painful than trying to play soccer with sore feet. Look for shoes at a shoe swap during registration when the kids are young, and ask the coaches and teammates what make of shoes they recommend. There can be a huge price difference among shoes.

Another piece of equipment that must be worn is shin pads. Shin pads are a small price to pay to protect a very sensitive area on the body, and are now standard equipment at all playing levels. They are small, curved pads that fit under the socks that protect the shins from kicks. Some have elastic and Velcro straps to help hold them in place, others have ankle protectors attached, and still others are single pieces of foam with plastic covers that are held in place by the socks alone. All of them are legal.

 Your child's uniform and other equipment needs somewhere to go after a game, especially when soaking wet or muddy. The most obvious place is into a gym bag. Rain gear can be invaluable in your child's gym bag. Even if it's not raining outside, a waterproof rain jacket is good for sitting on damp grass, or wrapping up muddy boots and uniforms after the game. Keep a towel or two, spare socks and a change of clothes in a plastic bag, especially if you have far to go after a rainy game.

Sports tape is always a good idea to have on hand. Shin pads can break, or shoes fall apart at the most inopportune moment, and it's tape to the rescue. It also comes in handy for taping jewelry like rings and bracelets which don't come off (even though they are supposed to) during a game. Players aren't permitted to wear any jewelry on the field as a safety precaution. In terms of additional padding for personal protection, nothing is required; however, boys may choose to wear a jock-strap, and older girls a sports bra.

Other safety equipment that is recommended but optional includes mouthguards and goggles if contact lenses are impossible. If your child does wear contacts, have an extra set and saline on hand because it's virtually impossible to find a lost lens in the grass.

Goalkeepers may choose from a range of special clothing. None of these is necessary, but as children's skills develop and shots get more power behind them and are more precisely placed, the physical demands on the goalkeeper increase. The first piece of equipment he will likely be interested in is gloves. There are many styles of gloves – some have padding, others have rubberized palms – all of which are legal. When glove shopping, try to find a pair that fits well. Wearing gloves that are too big is more of a handicap than wearing no gloves at all. Secondly, the goalkeeper may be interested in special padded shorts or leggings. This is to protect the sides of the hips as the goalkeeper makes an outstretched dive for the ball, and gives additional warmth on cold days. Sometimes goalkeepers are permitted to wear peaked caps (like baseball caps), but they aren't recommended. They may also wish to wear knee pads or elbow pads, but these usually hamper their ability to move around, and are usually discouraged. All that remains is the goal-keeper uniform, which is typically a long-sleeved and very distinctive (read "loud") shirt, and plain black or regulation striped shorts. The rules state the goalkeeper's shirt must be different from both teams' shirts, so designers have run amok and created some unusual designs in bizarre color combinations. Many leagues do not provide goalkeeper shirts, so if your child decides that playing in goal is the position for her, you may find yourself shirt shopping in no time.

There is one other recommended piece of equipment, and that is a soccer ball. The more exposure your child has to a ball the better. Having a good regulation size ball just hanging around the house to fool around with can provide more skill training than two practices a week. A regulation size ball for ages 11 and up is a size-five ball. The little ones use size-four or three balls, which are slightly smaller. Again, your budget may dictate how expensive a ball you get, but aim for a good ball of the proper weight. You can get cheaper balls but they are often heavy, and are unpleasant to kick, never mind receive with the head. One word of advice for all equipment, including the ball, is write your child's name on all of it with permanent marker. That way it stands less of a chance of disappearing.

CHAPTER SEVEN

The goalkeeper

There are many books written on soccer, but few of them deal with issues surrounding the goalkeeper. It is a unique position, and carries with it special responsibilities and sensibilities. So, here are a few words to help out, since everyone has to play goal sometime.

The goalkeeper is the last line of defense. She anchors the defence line, giving the team directions in terms of positioning and ball placement. She stands staunchly on her goal line, waiting for a ball to be fired at her, and to hurl her body in the way to prevent a goal from being scored. She is tough as nails, going into the thick of action, risking bone-crunching contact as she goes for the ball. She is a hawk, watching play develop, and adjusting her position to create a very narrow angle for advancing shooters. She has great timing and judgement, knowing when to be aggressive and rush out to get a ball, and when to hang back and wait. She is physically strong and tall, with confident hands and feet. She can kick the ball vast distances and to precise points on the field. And she knows the rules inside out, especially the rules that pertain to her. To sum up, the goalkeeper must be the wiliest and toughest player on the field.

PLAYING WITH THE HANDS

Let's start with the rules that pertain to the goalkeeper. First of all, the 18-yard box is her domain. She is able to use her hands to play the ball anywhere in this area, with the following exceptions: she may not play the ball with her hands if the ball is passed to her off the foot of one of her own players; nor may she handle the ball if she has played the ball with her own feet after controlling it with her hands. In other words, once she has picked up the ball, she cannot put it on the ground and pick it up again. She cannot juggle the ball with her feet and get it airborne, and catch it again with her hands. Once it's on the ground she must kick it.

If the ball is passed to her by one of her own players, she may only control the ball with her hands if the ball is passed off the player's head or knee or body part other than the foot. If it is deemed to be a controlled pass, the referee will call hand ball, and a direct free kick for the other team will result. (This rule is relatively new, and seems particularly nasty for the small fry who are just developing their ball control skills, but it *is* the rule.)

When within the goal area, a goalkeeper may use his hands to get control of the ball, or save a shot. Once this has been done, and the goalkeeper has possession of the ball, the ball is considered dead. Opposing players must then give the goalkeeper space to put the ball back into play. To do that, the goalkeeper may elect to kick the ball from his hands, or throw the ball to a teammate, or put the ball on the ground and kick it from there. He also has the option of putting the ball on the ground and dribbling it as far as he likes, bearing in mind that once out of the goal area, he can no longer play the ball with his hands. What he cannot do is walk around with the ball in his hands. He has four steps, *and four steps only*, to carry the ball before he gets rid of it. If he takes more, the opposing team gets an indirect free kick from the 18-yard line.

These rules can feel like cruel and unusual punishment to the inexperienced. It's always a tense moment after a save because no one knows for certain if the goalkeeper will be able to put the ball back into play properly. A high degree of skill, knowledge and confidence is needed to do it.

Like other players on the field, the goalkeeper cannot say "mine" or "my ball" when calling for the ball. He must use his own name or call "keeper's ball," or some such other identifying call. If he does yell "I've got it" or "mine," an indirect free kick will result! This is a disaster of course (but helps everyone to remember the rule for a LONG time).

STRATEGY AND THE GOALKEEPER

The wall

If a free kick is called in or around the goal area, the goal-keeper and the defense must act quickly to get a wall organized. The purpose of the wall is to cut down the amount of space a goalkeeper has to cover (or the target area a kicker has to aim at).

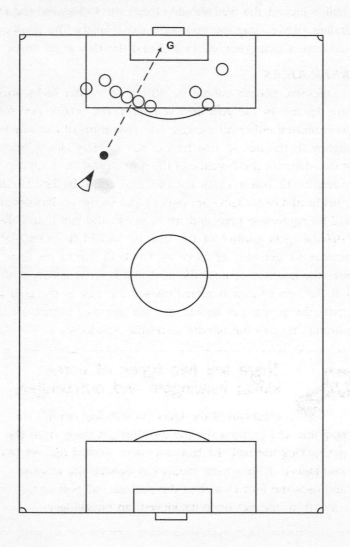

The goalkeeper and the defense work together to get the angle and position of the wall just right. To do that, the sweeper lines up between the ball and one of the posts of the net. The other players fall into place beside her, and the goalkeeper covers the remaining space in the net. All defensive players must stand 10 yards from the ball, with three to five players in the wall, and the others marking up one-on-one with offensive players, keeping them as far away from the goal as possible (players can be offside on free kicks). As the ball is kicked, the wall should charge the kicker, and the other defending players stay on their offensive players. The goalkeeper should have a clear view of the ball and the kick at all times.

CORNER KICKS

Offensive players cannot be offside on corner kicks, so one-on-one defense in the goal area is a must. The goalkeeper should position himself either on the goal line, two-thirds of the way back, or slightly in the net, so that he can see the ball clearly. Standing back two-thirds of the distance of the goal allows the goalkeeper to run towards the ball to catch it, rather than try to backpeddle if it's over his head. Corner kicks are direct kicks, so the goalkeeper really should be aggressive here, and try to get to the ball first. If he, or the defense, gets control of the ball, he should be yelling at his teammates to "get out," or move up the field, out of his area. This relieves the pressure around the goal, and is exercising the offside trap. If the corner kick is aimed toward the top of the goal area, as a pass, the goalkeeper should also yell "get out," as this is a great opportunity to trap the offense in offside positions.

There are two types of corner kicks: inswingers and outswingers.

Generally, if the kicker is standing behind the goal line and is using the the foot furthest away from the net to kick the ball, the ball will curve toward the net (an inswinger). If he or she stands just outside the sideline and uses the foot closest to the net, the ball will curve away from the net once it's kicked (an outswinger).

GOAL KICKS

With young kids goal kicks can be tricky. They don't have the power to kick the ball a long way, which is what you want to do on a goal kick. If the goalkeeper is the best kicker on the team, it's probably a good idea to have him take the kick, as long as a defensive player goes back into the goal to cover for him. This player can't use his hands, but he's a warm body to have there, just in case something goes wrong. Interestingly, goal kicks can be among the most nail-biting moments of the game, because something going wrong is almost inevitable. The goalkeeper needs to look sharp, and be prepared for the defense to intercept and come charging right back at him. It's usually a good idea to get the goal kickoff to the sidelines as soon as possible, so that the offense doesn't have too much time to mark up. A new rule allows goal kicks to happen anywhere along the six-yard line, regardless of which side of the goal the ball went out, and if the goalkeeper is watching the other team carefully, he'll play the ball to their weakest side, or switch sides to shake things up.

PENALTY SHOTS

The penalty shot is the single most nerve-wracking event of any game. It's a one-on-one duel, and the goalkeeper is the most disadvantaged. She must stand with both feet, still, on the goal line, at the time the ball is kicked. If she moves, and no goal is scored, another kick may be awarded. The skills involved here are manifold. She must analyze the kicker's positioning and approach to the ball to try to determine to which side of the goal it will go. She should NOT look at the kicker's eyes or head, nor should she focus too much on the stomach or hips. The most important thing is the BALL. The timing of the save is critical, and usually involves a flat-out dive to the side. If the ball is stopped, the goalkeeper should try to control it as fast as possible, because it is "live" and play can continue. If there's a big rebound, it usually spells big trouble. A defensive player should be ready to follow the kicker in, but because he has to stand 10 yards back, he's at a real disadvantage. The best thing that can happen is for the goalkeeper to charge after the ball until she has it squeezed solidly in her arms.

THE GOALKEEPER'S MIND

The goalkeeper's mental outlook is really the backbone of her performance on the field. Just because she's the last line of defense doesn't mean she's defensive in her attitude towards the game. Instead just the opposite is true; in soccer, the best defense can be good offense. The goalkeeper needs to be assertive in her play. It is usually a mistake to hang back on the goal line waiting for a shot to come. By coming off the line, the goalkeeper can cut down on the angle available for scoring, or force an error by intimidating the offensive player. On corner kicks and free kicks she should own the ball, fighting off all others for it. She needs great focus and concentration, not to mention determination to do her job. These traits should be fostered in your child. The more self-confidence she possesses, the better she will function in the goal crease.

This level of self-confidence becomes even more critical when she is scored against. Tears are not uncommon after the ball goes by the goaltender. Teammates need to be encouraged not to blame the goalkeeper when this happens, since the other team did manage to get by 10 of *them* before the goalkeeper ever saw action. But even when the team is supportive, a goalkeeper can feel badly and needs special support before the game, at half-time and afterwards. After she is scored against, she needs to be able to shake it off, relax and get ready for play to begin again. She will have success doing this if she is confident in her skills, her knowledge of the game and the support she gets from her team, the coach, other parents and her family.

CHAPTER EIGHT

Developing the basic skills at home

There are lots of things to do at home besides work on soccer skills, so it may sometimes be necessary to give your child a little nudge towards the soccer ball. Or it may be impossible to get him to put it away. It's important to see if your child is developing a real passion for the sport. You'll know it if the ball is crashing around the house all the time. If that's what's happening, then you definitely have a vested interest in developing your child's soccer skills. It will really save on the china.

If he's rather more content to stay glued to the television, then you've got a bit of a challenge ahead of you. Whichever child is closer to yours, you should know that the more the child does at home to develop his skills the better he will be. There is no substitute for practice, practice, practice.

If your child wants to work at his soccer skills, there are plenty of things he can do on his own, but it's better to have someone to work with. That someone can be you! There's no need to be a soccer whiz to help your child work on his skills at home. The following games and exercises are designed to be simple and fun, and require little skill on your part. All that you need to do is recognize when it's time to set the bar a little bit higher, or when it's time to knock it down a notch.

RUNNING

There's no escaping it. Some people are natural athletes and others are not. What does that mean? It means that some people can run with grace and ease without thinking about it. Their arms pump coordinated with their legs, they are relaxed as they move, they are completely balanced and in control of their limbs. Others look clumsy as they move. There is no rhythm to their movements – even walking can look like an effort. Their limbs look like they are fighting against each other and the body they are attached to. There is a constant strain to complete the skill or movement they are trying to execute. Most of us are somewhere in between these two extremes. Running may feel completely natural for some people, but it certainly doesn't for everyone – soccer players included. However, running is a necessary prerequisite for functioning on the soccer field. Youngsters need to be encouraged to work on developing their coordination in running. When playing outdoors, encourage games like tag and hide 'n' seek. These games develop speed and agility. One such game is Cat and Mouse.

Cat and Mouse

Cat and Mouse is a tag game that involves a group of children, usually about 12 or so, but you can play with fewer. Children should choose partners and spread out around the space with them. Partners need to face each other and hold hands. These pairs now form mouseholes. One pair now needs to be identified as the cat and the mouse. Just point to one child and say, "You're the mouse!" She should take off as quickly as she can, away from her partner, who is the cat. The cat chases the mouse until the mouse is touched. When that happens the roles switch, so the mouse becomes the cat, and the cat becomes the mouse. The only way to avoid being tagged is for the mouse to pop into a mousehole. The person who is looking at the mouse's back becomes the new mouse and needs to run away in a big hurry to avoid being tagged by the cat! It's a great party game and it needs little in the way of supervision. The only rules are to play safe and make sure everyone has a turn being the cat. It's a great game for developing speed, agility, observing and making quick decisions.

If you don't have a gang of kids around to play Cat and Mouse, it's easy to find an excuse to get your child to run as fast as she can. Have a toy or other object ready as an incentive or a reward for sprinting to goal. Instil a love of movement and running in your child by making everyday tasks into games. Laundry, repairing bicycles, cleaning house, all kinds of everyday tasks can turn into athletic enterprises. What you don't want to do is to start a training camp. Children do not need to work on cardiovascular conditioning, or to have a rigid training schedule. They should develop conditioning and agility through play. Only when they are older do they need to be concerned with Z-drills and running laps around the field. The key with youngsters is to be creative and have fun!

TRAPPING

The trap is a ball-control skill. You will need to have some type of ball or soft object to work on trapping. You may use a bean bag, a stuffed toy, a balled up pair of socks, or even a pillow to practice trapping. Just make sure you don't use your best throw pillows - things are bound to get a little beat up.

The self toss

Your youngster can work on trapping with the feet and legs on his own. He can toss the "ball" into the air and control it with his feet, his thigh and his lower abdomen. He can toss it straight up into the air in front of him and, once those traps are mastered, he can toss the ball to the side, further and further away from himself, and run to get it (trap it) before it hits the ground.

Partner play

The other way of practicing trapping is to work with your child. Be specific about the body part you want her to trap the ball with. That means the toss you give will have to be fairly accurate. When tossing a ball towards a youngster use a controlled, underhand toss thrown with two hands. Stand one to two metres away facing the player, making sure she's watching and in the ready position before tossing the ball. When making the toss make sure the ball has some loft to it and that there is no spin on the ball. To do that, toss the ball so that it goes up as it goes towards the youngster. The highest point of the toss should be the midpoint between you and your partner. Don't be embarrassed if you don't get it right the first few times. The controlled underhand toss is a very difficult skill to master. Once your youngster can control a ball that is tossed lightly to her, you can increase the distance between you and you can increase the speed of the ball. Don't move on to greater levels of difficulty until the child has mastered the skill.

The ready position is a standing position with the feet placed one slightly behind the other, the weight leaning slightly forward, the knees bent and the arms held slightly away from the body, elbows bent. The body should be relaxed and the player should be focused on the ball, or the relevant person or body part that she is about to interact with.

DRIBBLING

For dribbling your child really will need a ball. He should play with the ball, practicing with pylons or other obstacles. You can set up a type of obstacle course in the yard or park which he can negotiate around. Have him use the instep, the top of the foot and the outside of the foot when going around a pylon or obstacle. He should have a sense of mischief when dribbling. It's all about maintaining control of the ball when challenged, moving the ball in the direction one wants it to go, and getting out of tricky situations. One must be somewhat sly and devious to be a good dribbler – it's a mental game more than anything. Encouraging these attitudes in your child can be a fun thing, as long as you define the boundaries and remind him it's only for play. You can have a lot of fun by being the stooge, and having your child try to feint around you.

Another good dribbling partner is the family dog. Because dogs have a low center of gravity, they are extremely agile. They also love to play with balls and children. Pick a starting point for your child and have him try to dribble the ball to an end point. To make it more difficult have him dribble to the end with the dog touching the ball twice, or three times. Let them ham it up for as long as they can stand it. Your child may start to get frustrated because the dog is a huge obstacle. Dogs can always get to the ball faster and with greater ease than we can. They also have a tendency to pick the ball up and trot away with it. So watch for your child's frustration level getting too high, and end the game while it's still fun.

KICKING

When developing kicking skills, it's important for your child to work on accuracy before power, and to start with short distances and work up to longer distances. That way it's easier to get rid of the toe hack and to develop the proper techniques for passing and shooting. Also, start with static kicks and passes, keeping the ball on the ground. It's easier to receive the ball, control it and pass it off when it's on the ground. Once the pass on the ground is conquered using all three parts of the foot, work with your child on getting the ball into the air and being accurate at the same time. To increase the skill level needed, work on two-touch passing (a trap, then a pass), then one-touch passing (passing and controlling the incoming ball at the same time).

The wall pass

A fun game for your youngster to try is the wall pass. All he needs is a ball and a wall. Running along the wall, dribbling the ball, he should pass the ball to the wall. He needs to aim approximately 45 percent ahead of him. To help him out, you could draw a spot on the wall (use sidewalk chalk or other washable or temporary marker). He should run three paces, then make the pass. The ball should bounce off the wall and arrive further ahead so that it meets up with him a little further along the wall.

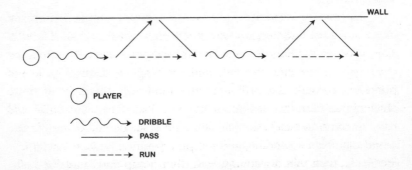

Your child should be encouraged to use both the inside of the foot furthest away from the wall and the outside of the foot nearest the wall to make and receive the passes. Set a reasonable goal in terms of the number of passes completed.

A fun way to work on shooting is to construct a small net at which to shoot, or use a hockey net. Standing no more than two metres from the net, your child can work on developing her power. She needs to work on planting her support foot in the right place (just behind and slightly to the side of the ball), getting her knee over the ball and powering through the ball, keeping the toes pointed and using a high follow-through. You can play a game with her where you tell her which corner to aim at when shooting, and give her points for every time she hits that corner. You can up the ante by taking points away if she misses the net from such close quarters. As she gets more advanced, she can decide whether or not she is going to shoot, or if she is going to fake a shot and then deliver a push pass. As you watch her, try to guess what she's going to do. If you guess right, you get a point. If you guess wrong, she gets a point. The object is to have her try to trick you with her body language, facial expression, arm position and drive towards the ball.

HEADING

A good place to practice heading is at home. Just remember, heading practice should be short, otherwise your child will have a ringing head for hours afterwards. Try to alternate it with some other activity.

To practice heading, put a ball or pillow, or other soft object into a small net and hang the net free from obstacles at head height. This way your child can practice the proper stance, keeping the eyes open as he hits the ball, and working on leaning back and punching through the ball with the forehead. To make it more challenging, raise the height of the net. That way your child will have to jump to head the ball. Once he is successful at hitting the raised ball from a standing and jumping position, he can start a few feet back, then take a running start, then jump and head the ball.

If you don't have anywhere to hang such an object, you can be the official ball or pillow holder. Just hold the pillow in the air at head height, and have your child head it away. You'll need to move your hand away so you don't hit his head. Then you can try tossing the pillow in the air. Have your child head the ball straight through, so it hits the ground right in front of him. Then you can work on changing the direction of the ball so that it goes straight downwards, or sideways. These exercises are much more advanced. Make sure that your child is strong and has mastered the straight-through header before moving on. The sideways header involves the use of the neck, shoulder and stomach muscles, and should wait until your child has a fairly developed skeletal and muscular system. Just remember, the most important principles in heading are to keep the eyes open and on the ball and to make sure the player hits the ball, rather than letting the ball hit the player.

GOALKEEPER SKILLS

The goalkeeper has a special set of soccer skills that need to be developed in addition to those of regular field players. These can be worked on at practice while the others are off running, but it's best if the goalkeeper participates as much as possible in drills with the others. Since there is only one goalkeeper on a team, it's very difficult to find another team player with whom to practice a goalkeeper's special drills. As a parent, however, you can help your child develop goalkeeper skills by trying some of the following:

Stretching and falling

Most kids are afraid of playing in goal because they're afraid of getting hurt. You can remove some of these fears by building confidence and developing skills in non-game situations. Before any practice session, it's important to warm up the muscles first by jogging or cycling or doing jumping jacks. Then there should be a stretching session when the large muscle groups and joints are stretched, flexed and rotated. Goalkeepers should take care to stretch their necks, backs, shoulders, arms, wrists and fingers, so they are good and warm.

Once your child is warmed up and stretched, you can work on scooping and protecting the ball with the arms and shoulders.

He should always be encouraged to meet the ball, moving towards it, bending and scooping. Start with short passes along the ground, then short bouncing passes, and then after several hours, weeks or months, you may graduate to harder shots. The most important thing is to make the beginner goalkeeper confident in his ability to control the ball and not be afraid of it.

Kids can learn to be unafraid of falling by starting low to the ground. Beginning in a sitting position, have the child stretch his arms out fully above his head, breathe in, and fall over onto his side, breathing out as he lands. Once comfortable with this, he can move up to his knees. It's important to emphasize that he stretch out his arms and rib cage, and to protect his head as he lands by cradling it on his shoulder. You can add a ball at any time after he's comfortable falling. Don't do this exercise too long – maybe five or six falls per side, then go on to something else.

Other skills that can be worked on include throwing, punching or lifting a ball backwards and upwards over the head, punting, drop kicking, sliding low to get a ball, and jumping high to catch a ball. Start slowly, with light tosses, and work on getting a high success ratio before moving on to a higher level of difficulty. Remember, any work you do with your budding goalkeeper should be fun and geared towards making him confident and unafraid.

DEVELOPING A POSITIVE ATTITUDE

Playing competitive sports can contribute to one's enjoyment of life in immeasurable ways. The overall health benefits go well beyond the physical, and enhance your child personally in every aspect of day-to-day life.

Like most team sports, soccer involves both individual skills and team skills. Children can be quite solitary in their pursuit of excellence in soccer. Encouraging them to take a ball, play with it and work with it, teaches them self-sufficiency, independence and focus on tasks. These days, attention spans appear to be shortening, and any exercise of this mental faculty is valuable. Ball juggling, dribbling, and mastering different types of passes and shots take a high degree of concentration, and all can be done on one's own. In addition, watching and studying the game of soccer can be of benefit to children. Going out on a Saturday afternoon to watch the local rep or semipro team is not only fun, but allows children to see how play develops, and what skill levels can be attained. Failing that, soccer is featured on Saturday morning television, and kids should be encouraged to take in a game or two that way. It is often a valuable window on the world, and can give some insight into other cultures, where soccer is a national obsession and people are much more enthusiastic about the games than we are in Canada.

While the above activities can be pursued alone, it's often more fun and beneficial to join your child in some of them. Showing your own understanding and enjoyment of the game will encourage youngsters to play. They enjoy play-time with their parents, and will value the practice all the more for your company. Furthermore, you can help to teach each other about the game, and talk about strategy as you watch a game together. Depending on how much time has passed since your child's last game, it may be valuable to talk about key moments in the game, and to discuss alternative plays that could have helped the team out. It's not recommended that you strike up this conversation five minutes after a dreadful loss, however; wait a couple of days for the emotions to subside, then do your post-game analysis in a calm and intellectual way.

The element of team play is one that is increasingly valued. It is not so much taught, but experienced and developed in an organic way. While leadership in individuals is valuable in many ways on the soccer field, it cannot win games with any consistency. Soccer players must learn to trust and rely on their teammates. This lesson is one of the first to learn in soccer, and the sense of freedom it gives is inspiring. The beauty of the game of soccer is the pass. To develop team play to such a high level that players can move almost instinctively to places where they can give and receive passes with ease, is the essence of the game. The shot on goal is the final pass, the culmination of successful team play, and is the symbol of everyone's hard work. It is almost as good to assist in a goal as to score it, and the most satisfying goals are those that are scored in the flow of the game. (Penalty shots and free kicks are nice, but it usually means somebody suffered to get them. The spirit isn't quite the same when a team scores that way.) Of course, the magic passes don't develop accidentally, or while in some sort of trance. They are the product of lots of practice, and good old-fashioned co-operation.

As part of team play, young players need to be encouraged to talk to each other on the field. They need to work on small passes where they direct each other around the field. This activity not only teaches strong communication skills, but also the ability to give and take direction from one's peers, to respect one's teammates and to develop the ability to work together toward a common goal. These values will serve players well throughout their lives.

CHAPTER NINE

Soccer around the world

Legend has it that soccer or football began in medieval times, when rival bands living in what is now known as England began kicking the skulls of their enemies around on the ground. It is also rumored that the Chinese played a similar game during the Han Dynasty, and that the Greeks and Romans enjoyed kicking a ball about on a fine Saturday as well. Soon after travellers of British descent landed on North American shores, it seems the first international match broke out – the crew of the *HMS Sunneshine* versus the Inuit of Gilbert Sound. The rest, as they say, is history.

THE HISTORY OF SOCCER IN CANADA

Within a couple hundred years or so, some British soldiers stationed at St. John's, Newfoundland, were staging matches against out-of-towners, and before anyone knew it the sport had been exported to all the major port cities in Canada. In Ottawa, Montreal and Toronto, various athletic societies and grammar schools took up the game with vigor, and in the 1870s it became the number one winter sport at Queen's University. Still in its rudimentary form and without a great many rules, the game found itself heading westward. One of University of Toronto's first players took up a teaching position in Berlin (Kitchener) and, together with two other colleagues, established the region as one of the strongest in soccer in Canada. By 1901 teams from four different leagues around the province were competing for the provincial championship in four separate age categories.

The Hudson's Bay Company imported as well as exported. Soccer matches became an established tradition with the men of the Hudson's Bay Company, starting with games against the British sailors that came to pick up furs and drop off goods for delivery across the country. With posts across the nation it wasn't long before the game had taken root from coast to coast. Adding to its popularity were the North West Mounted Police squads, who played regularly through the mid-1800s; in fact, the Saskatchewan Football (Soccer) League was formed in 1875. Calgary formed its first "football" club in 1888, as did Lethbridge in 1889. By 1914 there were no fewer than 60 soccer clubs in the Calgary area.

The settlers of Newfoundland were regularly competing against the French of St. Pierre and Miquelon throughout the late 1800s, but the first official international match took place in St. Louis in 1884, where the Western Football Association Selects trounced the St. Louis Thistles 9-0 on Christmas day. After that several international competitions took place, usually with the Canadian squads emerging victorious.

By 1912 there was an increasing desire for a national championship and national organization. The Dominion of Canada Football Association was formed, and in that same year applied for membership in FIFA. At the request of the DCFA, the Governor-General became the patron of the national championship game and the Connaught Cup was born. In 1926 the Connaught Cup was retired and the new Challenge Cup was played for – emblematic of the senior amateur championship in Canada – and is still played for today.

By the 1930s and '40s soccer had a great deal of competition – both from other sports, such as hockey and football, and from financial and geopolitical pressures. It suffered a sudden lapse in popularity. World War II proved a serious blow to the sport, and it took years of hard work and reorganizing to bring soccer back to its place as a premier school and club-driven sport in Canada. It wasn't until the 1970s that the game caught on again in a very big way, but once it took hold, soccer was hugely popular across the country. Over half a million Canadian youth are now enrolled in soccer programs, and the numbers continue to grow every year.

Out of these rather gruff and shaky beginnings, a game of grace and skill has evolved which is enjoyed by millions around the world, both as fans and players. The international governing body is the Fédération Internationale de Football Association (FIFA). Located in Zurich, Switzerland, the FIFA council generates all the rules associated with the modern game, and oversees many international tournaments. The international road map of soccer is very complex, but here are a few highlights in the history of the world's most popular sport.

THE WORLD CUP

The World Cup is the premier event in soccer, and indeed rivals the Olympics for national and international prestige. Held every four years, national teams composed of each country's best players compete for the honor of the world title. Held since 1930, the tournament has expanded from 13 teams to 24, with a complicated process of continental qualifying matches held in the 18 months prior to the tournament. The newest additions include teams from Africa and Asia, notably Cameroon and Korea, and the United States. But the world powers in soccer have consistently proven themselves to be from Europe and South America. They include Germany, England, Brazil, Italy and Argentina. The 1994 World Cup was held in the United States, and was considered a huge success. Little violence on or off the field, lots of media coverage and many close games made the perfect mix. Soccer became firmly planted in the North American psyche, and has now become the most-played participation sport in Canada, and the number one sport played by American women. For males it ranks second, just behind basketball.

THE FA CUP

The game most resembling soccer as we now know it came into existence in 1863 after 11 of London, England's schools and clubs met to create the English Football Association, and devise a formal set of rules that differentiated soccer from rugby. Indeed, the term "soccer" itself was born at this time, as opposed to "rugger," arising from the "soc" in association. From this federation grew several more, including Scotland, Ireland and Wales' own associations. These bodies got together to further standardize the rules, and to compete for the British championship in the 1880s.

The FA Cup was first devised in 1872, and was to be a single-elimination tournament that any club could enter. That tradition, among others, holds true today. The competition has expanded from 15 entrants in the first tournament, to 73 in 1882, to 242 in 1901. The current tournament allows 256 teams to compete annually for the coveted Challenge Cup. Perennial powerhouses include Manchester United, Liverpool and Arsenal, although competition is getting tighter and tighter.

AROUND THE WORLD

FIFA

Soccer was increasingly exported out of Britain to the Caribbean, South America and Europe, and soon the countries around the world wanted to participate in international competition. In 1904 the Fédération Internationale de Football Association was formed. This organization is the official governing body of soccer around the world and is responsible for drawing up the laws of the game, setting training programs for referees, overseeing international competitions of all types and hearing appeals. The International Board from Britain joined in 1905, and the first World Cup held under its auspices was held in 1930. There are 178 countries affiliated with FIFA, Canada among them.

UEFA

The European arm of FIFA is the Union of European Football Associations (UEFA). It organizes a number of prestigious tournaments as well. The Champions Cup is an international tournament that pits the professional league champions against one another. In 1961 another tournament was created for the amateur teams who had won their national championships; this is known as the Cup Winners Cup. For teams that don't qualify for those two competitions, there is also the UEFA Cup, which is held every year as well.

The Olympics

Soccer was a demonstration sport at the 1896 and 1900 Olympics, with champion clubs representing their countries. In 1904 it became a medal event in St. Louis, and for the first and last time in Olympic history a Canadian team took home the gold medal! Today most countries in the world compete in Olympic soccer competition. There is now women's competition as well as men's, and it is considered a highly prestigious tournament (but it doesn't carry the same mystique as the World Cup).

South America

Levels of competition similar to Europe occur in South America. The professional club champions meet in the Libertadores Cup each year. The winner of that goes on to play the Champions Cup winner (European professional champions) in the Toyota Cup in Japan. The amateur national championship teams go to the Copa America tournament, and from there to fight the Europeans for the Artemio Franchi Trophy.

North America

The North American soccer championship for men is called the Gold Cup, and didn't begin until 1991. The region includes North America, Central America and the Caribbean (CONCACAF). Professional and amateur players from these regions combine to form teams to compete. The top four teams from the CONCACAF will compete in the World Cup tournament. For amateur players the Under 20 World Youth Championship was created in 1977, then the Under 17 Championship in 1985 and the Women's World Championship in 1991.

Canada

The structure of competition in Canada is interesting. Most communities offer recreational or house-league soccer, either through the municipality or a local soccer club. From there the level of competition rises. Your child may prove himself a skilful player, and try out for a town all-star team, or club team, that competes regionally. Once he has claimed the regional championship, he may go on to compete for the provincial championship and, from there, to the Canadian championship tournament. After winning the Nationals, this team could go on to represent Canada at the World Youth Championships.

Another route to international play is to be invited to try out for one of the provincial teams, which only plays interprovincially and in international tournaments; from there, a player may be invited to try out for the national team, which is the team that represents the country at the CONCACAF Gold Cup. This team may also be made up of professional and college or university players who are Canadians. And if the player is a member of this team and they do well in Gold Cup competition, then it's on to the World Cup.

Now, before you get too excited, you should know that even though the modern Canadian team has done better and better in international competition, it has a way to go before getting into the World Cup finals. At least, that's the way it is for men. The Canadian Women's team has done considerably better, finishing in the top ten in Women's World Cup competition.

THE WOMEN'S WORLD CHAMPIONSHIPS

The first-ever Women's World Cup was held in 1991 in Guangzhou, China. The stadium was filled with 60,000 fans to watch the U.S. narrowly defeat Norway in the final. The second world cup saw Norway face off against Brazil for world supremacy, with the Norwegians emerging victorious. The world powers in women's soccer are the United States, China, Taiwan, Norway, Sweden and Brazil. There is very little to distinguish the women's game from the men's. The pace and playmaking levels are identical. There may be a slight power differential, and of course the amount of money involved is much more limited, but otherwise, it's the same game! Currently soccer is the premier women's sport in North America, and still growing in popularity. While most players are amateurs several professional leagues have started up, primarily in Asia. Players are drafted and paid salaries, just like the large men's leagues. There is currently a big push on in the U.S. to form a professional league. With the 1999 World Cup being held there, the organizers see it as a very exciting time for female athletes of all types.

AH, POPULARITY!

Soccer continues to be the most popular game in the world. In fact, its popularity is increasing and, with the exposure the game recently received in the United States from hosting the World Cup, it's likely to explode in communities across the United States and Canada. Although several professional franchises and leagues have started and sputtered in North America, there is a renewed interest in professional soccer here. Currently there are several Canadian teams playing in the A League against American teams. The Toronto

Lynx, the Montreal Impact, the Edmonton Drillers and the Vancouver 86ers are the current professional franchises. Television coverage of both professional and amateur teams is increasing, with the road to the World Cup being closely followed by TSN and local cable stations. The American cable sports channel ESPN has recently signed a multi-year deal together with ABC to broadcast a number of soccer games. With increased media coverage in North America it is hoped that increased fan support will result.

Some critics have said that soccer makes terrible television, and to a certain extent this may be true. The pace and spread-out nature of the game doesn't lend itself to stationary camera positions where a player can be kept in frame for a long period of time. The path and direction of the ball is highly unpredictable, which makes it necessary to rely on the high and wide camera angles that are frequently seen. North American audiences are used to being up close and personal with their sports, and right in the thick of the action. However, this is the challenge for the mighty television professionals, as well as for us audience members. Remember, if you find it disappointing on TV, you and your child can always go see it live! The success of professional soccer will continue to depend on the level of support each team receives in its community, and this means everyone involved in the game.

CHAPTER TEN

Sportsmania

Because soccer is popular in so many nations around the world, and each nation is so completely zealous in its belief that soccer is ITS GAME, each country has established its own way of recognizing its stars. Each nation has its roster of soccer heroes and legends that the children learn about in school, or via fanzines, magazines, newspapers and television. There are literally thousands of soccer magazines and books written in over forty different languages, as well as Web sites, movies and video games. The following is a selected list of titles that you and your child might find interesting, exciting and useful as you both delve deeper into the world of soccer.

BOOKS

There are hundreds of books written about soccer. Some are historical, some biographical, many skills and coaching related. Very few are fictional, and most are aimed at parents, older players and coaches. Your local library is a great place to start, as well as your provincial soccer association. Here a few books that are easy to understand, enthusiastic and helpful:

- *Go for the Goal! Techniques and Strategies for the Complete Soccer Player*, by Stuart Murray, Simon and Shuster, 1994.
  - Murray is a former semipro soccer player who has coached club, recreational league and high-school soccer for over 20 years. This fast-paced book is full of skills and drills, team play and historical information, presented in an easy-to-read, high-energy way that makes the author's enthusiasm for the game infectious.

- *Soccer Skills and Drills*, (Revised and Updated), by Gary Rosenthal, Simon and Shuster, 1994.
  - Rosenthal is a former all-star goalkeeper, professor of physical education and health at New York City Technical College of the City University of New York, and author of four books on soccer and volleyball. The book includes excellent drills to develop skills at all levels, but is aimed at the more advanced player.
- *Soccer Coaching Ages 5-12*, by Andrew Caruso, Soccer Coaching Press (Quakertown, Penn.), 1992.
- *The American Encyclopedia of Soccer*, by Zander Hollander, Everest House Publishers, 1980.
- *My Life and the Beautiful Game*, by Pele (Edson Arantes do Nascimento) with Robert Fish, Warner Books, 1977.
  - The greatest player of all time writes about his life and experiences in soccer. A book full of joy and a terrific story of the rise from nothing to international stardom.

MAGAZINES

There are only a few magazines published in Canada currently. Most of the soccer magazines we get are British, but of course every nation in South America and Europe has four or five magazines dedicated to following the game and its stars.

- *BBC Match of the Day Magazine* is a huge magazine from England with a ton of player profiles, columns, team updates ... you name it. Great photos and a somewhat frenetic layout give it pace and energy. It feels like a soccer game.
- *Football Europe* calls itself "Your essential guide to European Football," and it certainly gets you going in the right direction. Lots of commentary, action photos and all the standings.
- *Inside Soccer* is a smaller Canadian publication that looks at professional and amateur soccer in Ontario, provides coaching tips and discusses issues within Canadian soccer.
- *Shoot,* is a British creation, a very splashy magazine that covers events, players, scores and has columns galore. Lots of pull-out posters to hang up as well - which is great fun for the kids.

- *Soccer Canada* is the official magazine of the Canadian Soccer Association. It is published four times a year and is available through subscription and at bigger newsstands, or at the CSA or your provincial soccer association. Colorful and informative, it has its work cut out for it to challenge the hype of the British magazines.
- *Soccer Digest* is an American magazine that covers both amateur and professional soccer teams and players in the United States. A wide range of topics and issues are addressed, but you need to be a fan to get up to speed in a hurry.
- *World Soccer*, also a British publication, is dedicated to following professional soccer in Britain, Europe and around the world. Player profiles, event coverage and staying up-to-date with transfers are among its priorities. A very slick magazine.

VIDEOS

For the ultimate fan there are videos of practically every significant game played in Europe in the past 10 years. Or, at least it seems that way. The difficulty is obtaining them readily here in Canada. The best sources for European and South American game videos are the magazines listed above. Below are listed some of the popular coaching and training videos. They may be available through video distributors and retailers, but you will probably need to ask for a special order. Barring that, try your provincial soccer association, local club or soccer-supply store. Networking is the key to getting hold of the best titles.

- *Soccer Fundamentals with Wiel Coerver.* The soccer guru has produced a three-part coaching series on soccer fundamentals. Technically proficient, highly motivating and proven effective, these are great watching for parents and kids alike.
- *Sports Clinic Soccer.* An 80-minute session with Herbert Vogelsinger, former NASL coach and developer of champion players.
- *Head to Toe: Soccer for Junior Players.* A very good video on soccer basics for beginning players, coaches and parents.

- *Soccer with Bob Gansler*. Former Olympic coach Gansler demonstrates all the key skills. This solid ESPN produced video is aimed at more developed players and builds confidence and a solid soccer foundation.

WEB SITES

There are now hundreds of Web sites that follow sports around the world, and there are still more dedicated to soccer exclusively. The following is a selected bibliography of fun and informative Web sites for kids and adults. But beware – you can spend hours delving into the world of soccer on the net. There are just so many places to visit!

The Canadian Soccer Association:
http://canoe5.canoe.ca/SoccerCanada

World Soccer:
http://worldsoccer.miningco.com

FootballNet:
www.futurenet.com/footballnet

Planet Soccer:
http://planet-soccer.com

College Soccer Weekly:
http://www.collegesoccer.com

Once in any of these Web sites, you can link to others. Some of the best are:

Dutch Teletext Guide
The Daily Soccer
Soccer Features
ESPNET Sportzone
Soccer America Online
Soccernet
When Saturday Comes (WSC)

GAMES

The most old-fashioned soccer-related game is *foosball*. This is a table game similar to table hockey. There is a box approximately three by four feet and eight inches deep, with six poles running through it widthwise. On these poles little wooden players are mounted so that the pole runs through their torsos. The players are suspended on the poles so that they can spin around freely. The poles are also several inches wider than the box so that the players can move side to side. For each team one pole holds the goalkeeper, another pole holds two or three defenders, and the third pole holds three or four forwards. Each team's players overlap one another, so that the arrangement looks like this: team A goalkeeper, team A defense, team B forwards, team A forwards, team B defense, team B goalkeeper.

To play the game two, four or six people control the poles from outside the box. A small wooden ball is dropped into the center of the box and the game commences. Players suspended on poles twirl around attempting to pass the ball up to the forward line and then twirl to take a shot on net. Defenders are twirled around to intercept passes. There's a fast flurry of activity in a foosball game, and sometimes it can get pretty intense. Foosball tables are hard to come by in Canada, but should be obtainable at specialty sports stores. The best way to get one is to make one.

There are many soccer-related games on the Internet to be played. Some of them revolve around managing teams, others are betting games. In terms of betting – beware – the bets are real. Some of these are:

- *Extra Time* – a team managing game with a weekly fee
- *Football Manager Games* – a game that is free to download, where players manage teams and compete in world competition
- *The Golden League* – a fantasy league based on real players' stats
- *The Ladder Electronic Football League* – might be good, but has a yearlong waiting list
- *Major League Soccer Manager* – a simulation game that is free to download

- *Football betting with Zetters* – a real and legal betting game based in England

There are also videogames on the market that get more realistic and sophisticated every year. Check your local electronics or computer store to find the latest and greatest.

SOCCER CAMPS

There are many sport and soccer camps springing up across the country. Many are by invitation only, but some are open to anyone. These camps offer fairly intensive training for players, focusing on skills and developing playmaking. Camps can be quite competitive and provide good training in the area of mental toughness. There is usually time for good fun, but participants need to know that they are there to train and learn.

To find out about camps in your area contact your local soccer club or league, and keep an eye out for advertisements in your local paper and the Canadian soccer magazines.

SOCCER ASSOCIATIONS

A valuable source of information about leagues, supplies, books and videos is your provincial soccer association. Below is the vital information to get you started.

FIFA
P.O. Box 85
8030 Zurich, Switzerland

The Canadian Soccer Association
Place Soccer Canada
237 Metcalfe Street
Ottawa, ON Canada   K2P 1R2
Web site: http://canoe5.canoe.ca/SoccerCanada

Alberta Soccer Association
c/o Commonwealth Stadium
11000 Stadium Road
Edmonton, AB   T5J 2R7
Web site: http:/www.albertasoccer.com
E-mail: soccer@telusplanet.net

B.C. Soccer Association
1126 Douglas Road
Burnaby, BC   V5C 4Z6

Manitoba Soccer Association
200 Main Street
Winnipeg, MB   R3C 4M2

Ontario Soccer Association
7601 Martingrove Road
Vaughan, ON   L4L 9E4
Web site: http://www.soccer.on.ca
E-mail: info@soccer.on.ca

Fédération Quebecoise de Soccer-Football
4545, Pierre-de-Coubertin
Montreal, PQ   H1V 3R2

Soccer New Brunswick
79 Hazen Avenue
Renforth, NB   E2H 1N9
E-mail: soccernb@nb.sympatico.ca

Soccer Nova Scotia
P.O. Box 3010 South
5516 Spring Garden Road
Halifax, NS   B3J 3G6

P.E.I. Soccer Association
Confederation Court Mall
Lower Level
P.O. Box 1863
Charlottetown, PEI   C1A 7K7

NWT Soccer Association
Box 336
Yellowknife, NWT   X1A 2N3
Web site: http://users.internorth.com/NWTSA

Yukon Soccer Association
Sport Yukon Building, 4061 – 4th Avenue
Whitehorse, YT   Y1A 1H1

Glossary

Attack A team is on the attack as soon as it takes possession of the ball. Team players turn the ball up the field and try to score a goal.

Charging The term used to describe tackling using the shoulder and leaning into the player with the ball. Too big a lean that turns into a push is an illegal charge.

Chip A short, lofted kick.

Corner kick An offensive, direct free kick taken from the corner of the field, resulting from the ball going out-of-bounds over the goal line and being last touched by a defending player.

Cross A pass from one side of the field into the center, or to the other side of the field.

Dangerous play A play where one or more players runs the risk of injury. It usually involves the foot getting close to the head; either the kicker or the player placing his head close to a kick may be called. The result is an indirect free kick.

Defender A player primarily responsible for defending his own goal, feeding the ball up to the halfbacks and forwards, and supporting them on the attack.

Direct kick	A dead ball kick that may be shot directly into the goal to score.
Dribbling	Using the feet in a series of short kicks to move the ball along the ground.
Drop ball	The method used to restart the game after an injury or mistaken call or other no-fault stoppage in play. Two players face each other while the referee drops the ball between them. They may only kick the ball after it has touched the ground.
Flick pass	A short pass taken with the outside of the foot.
Free kick	A kick taken to restart play after an infraction, the ball going out-of-bounds over the goal line, or a goal. See direct kick and indirect free kick.
Forward	A player primarily responsible for offense and scoring goals.
Goal	A team scores when the ball completely crosses the goal line between the goal's uprights and under the crossbar.
Goal kick	A kick taken from the six-yard line by the defending team after an offensive player kicks the ball out-of-bounds over the goal line.
Goal-side	The term used to explain the proper defensive positioning of players. It means they must place themselves between the opponents and their own net.
Halfback	The midfielder who connects offensive and defensive play. Halfbacks are the workhorses of the team who are playmakers as well as defenders.
Hand ball	An infraction resulting in a direct free kick when a player plays the ball with the hand or arm.

Indirect free kick	A dead ball kick taken to restart play after an infraction. The ball must be touched by another player before it can score a goal.
Kickoff	The method used to start the game and to restart play after a goal is scored. It is considered to be a direct kick.
Linesman	An official who runs along the sidelines (touch lines) who is responsible for calling the ball out-of-bounds, which team has possession of the ball, and offsides.
Marking	The term used to describe guarding an opponent.
Obstruction	An infraction when a player prevents another player from getting to the ball while making no attempt to get to the ball himself.
Offside	An infraction when an offensive player is sent a pass without there being two defenders between him and the goal line. One of the defenders may be the goalkeeper. There must be two defenders between the receiver and the goal line at the moment the ball is kicked.
Penalty kick	A direct free kick taken from a spot 12 yards out from the center of the goal. It is a one-on-one, one-time shot that is "live" after it is taken.
Penalty area	The box in front of the goal, 18 yards deep and 36 yards wide, that identifies the space where the goalkeeper may use her hands. Any serious infraction that a defender commits in this box results in a penalty shot.
Referee	The official on the field who keeps time, controls the play and is the final authority in running the game and interpreting rules.
Save	The term used when a goalkeeper prevents a goal from being scored.

Slide tackle	A desperation tackle when a player slides at the ball as it is being dribbled by an offensive player in order to knock it out of harm's way.
Striker	A forward, or attacker.
Support	A teammate on offense who follows behind the ball carrier to provide an outlet for a pass; or a teammate positioned as a backup to a player who is challenging an attacking player.
Sweeper	A player who plays behind the defensive line as a cover for challenging players.
Tackle	Using the feet and upper body to take the ball away from another player.
Throw-in	The method of restarting play after the ball goes out-of-bounds across the sideline. The player throwing the ball in must use two hands, on either side of the ball, lifting it overhead while keeping both feet on the ground.
Touch	The area that is out-of-bounds along the sidelines of the field.
Trap	Stopping the ball dead, or the moment of controlling it.
Volley	A kick taken while the ball is in flight.
Wall	A defensive play with several players standing in a line in front of a free kick in an attempt to cut down the available space in goal.
Wall Pass	A type of pass when a player passes the ball to a stationary target (teammate) who allows the ball to bounce directly off him and back to the original player. It is also known as a give-and-go pass.

**For fifty years, Coles Notes have been helping
students get through high school and university.
New Coles Notes will help get you through the rest of life.**

Look for these NEW COLES NOTES!

GETTING ALONG IN ...

- French
- Spanish
- Italian
- German
- Russian

HOW TO ...

- Write Effective Business Letters
- Write a Great Résumé
- Do A Great Job Interview
- Start Your Own Small Business
- Buy and Sell Your Home
- Plan Your Estate

YOUR GUIDE TO ...

- Basic Investing
- Mutual Funds
- Investing in Stocks
- Speed Reading
- Public Speaking
- Wine
- Effective Business Presentations

MOMS AND DADS' GUIDE TO ...

- Basketball for Kids
- Baseball for Kids
- Soccer for Kids
- Hockey for Kids
- Gymnastics for Kids
- Martial Arts for Kids
- Helping Your Child in Math
- Raising A Reader
- Your Child: The First Year
- Your Child: The Terrific Twos
- Your Child: Age Three and Four

HOW TO GET AN A IN ...

- Sequences & Series
- Trigonometry & Circle Geometry
- Senior Algebra with Logs & Exponents
- Permutations, Combinations & Probability
- Statistics & Data Analysis
- Calculus
- Senior Physics
- Senior English Essays
- School Projects & Presentations

**Coles Notes and New Coles Notes are available at the following
stores: Chapters • Coles • Smithbooks • World's Biggest Bookstore**

NOTES & UPDATES